Three Little Girls Lost

Gladys Lovell Gartrell

Bloomington, IN  Milton Keynes, UK

authorHOUSE™

AuthorHouse™
1663 Liberty Drive, Suite 200
Bloomington, IN 47403
www.authorhouse.com
Phone: 1-800-839-8640

AuthorHouse™ UK Ltd.
500 Avebury Boulevard
Central Milton Keynes, MK9 2BE
www.authorhouse.co.uk
Phone: 08001974150

This book is a work of non-fiction. Unless otherwise noted, the author and the publisher make no explicit guarantees as to the accuracy of the information contained in this book and in some cases, names of people and places have been altered to protect their privacy.

First published by AuthorHouse 7/7/2006

ISBN: 1-4259-4447-7 (sc)

Printed in the United States of America
Bloomington, Indiana

This book is printed on acid-free paper.

This book is dedicated to my sisters, Nancy and Dorothy, (Dot) who were with me in the beginning of my life and comforted me in the awful dark of many a horrific night.

And to Dave, my husband of 50 plus years, and my daughters, Roberta, and Peggy, who have been with me through the last.

Many years ago, even as a little girl, I think I had three ambitions for my life. I know they will not seem too ambitious to most people. The first one came true much sooner than I expected. I remember my Daddy telling me when I was 15 years old, "Gladys, you had better get out in the kitchen and learn to do some cooking." And I very seriously said "why? I'm not getting married until I'm 25".

My earliest memory seems to be when I was 2 years old. We were visiting at a friend's house in what is called "the valley" in El Paso. Being just a baby, probably still wearing a diaper, drooping around my ankles, I felt this awful pain in the left side of my face. The terrible pain and blood everywhere. I seem to remember being scooped up and taken to the hospital. William Beaumont hospital in El Paso. The doctor was very upset because no one knew the cause. There were guesses that maybe a sharp rock or maybe a dog had bit my face. All my baby teeth that I had were gone. My upper lip was torn open and the tear had gone all the way to the left corner of my eye. To this day, the muscles don't work in that side of my face. The year was 1938, the world was gearing up for what turned out to be World War II and the whole world was watching Adolph Hitler and his plans for domination of the world. Since my Daddy was in the army, the doctors were in the army, my face took second place in priority. The surgeons were planning plastic surgery, after I healed some. But fate happens. Japan changed all that on Dec. 7, 1941. So the whole base got moving and getting all of Fort Bliss ready to ship out on a moments notice. This included getting rid of the horses. I can still see the soldiers leading their own horse up the ramps leading to the stock cars standing on the tracks.

I had never seen grown men crying and these men did cry like babies because each man's horse was his lifeline to getting back to the fort. Of course, I didn't understand it all. My own Daddy was crying and standing as tall as the next man. Then we got word they were going on maneuvers and that scared me bad. I cried for days. It seemed nobody thought of the kids and never did any explaining. They went on maneuvers several times after that. Then came Japan. Then Fort Bliss got their ship out orders. Well, when I heard that, I was one happy little girl. I thought there would be no more maneuvers, which meant Daddy would be safe. After all, I was only 5 years old. Let me tell you, I never knew how lucky I was to just have worry about maneuvers.

My mother was left to take care of me and my 2 sisters. I was what was called the baby of the family. and the most inclined to go exploring. Didn't ever worry at that age that there were bad people out there...And it started in my own house. My mother was a very poor excuse for a mother. We girls went to bed many a night hungry, while she sat in the dining room entertaining her men friends. We were so hungry we would go out and hunt through garbage cans for scrapes of food... She didn't bathe us, comb our hair or feed us. The favorite thing was to send us to the movies. I would go to church to try to find love and companionship. That was another path I tried to follow.

The Red Cross got wind of our state of affairs and sent Daddy home from the South Pacific on a hardship leave. So the first thing that happened was my folks got a divorce. Never will I forget the judge asking me who I wanted to go with, my mother or my Dad, who had been gone for 4 years. Not a good idea. It split my loyalties.

And made me feel like a traitor no matter who I chose. So I refused to pick. The last day I saw my mother, she came out to Logan Heights to get her belongings. I just sat there feeling like I was dying. I have never felt that feeling before and hope I never do again. I was so melancholy. I'm sure this is what people feel when they end their lives. I didn't see my mother again for 42 years. A few letters over the years, but nothing serious.

My Daddy had a very hard time after that, trying to get over his war experiences and being stuck with 3 little girls to raise. He ran right out and found us a "mother". HA! She was full-blooded Mexican and meaner than a snake. The stunts she pulled on us, nobody would believe. We tried and tried to tell people about what was going on, but most didn't want to get involved. Daddy worked graveyard shift; he went to work at 11:00 P.M. By midnight, Rose, that was her name, had awakened us with the feeling of Dad's army belt coming down across our backs. Poor Nancy, my oldest sister, really got it bad. Then when Rose got tired of beating Nancy, she turned on Dorothy, who we called Dot. That would go on for about 45 minutes to an hour. Well, guess what? Then it was my turn. Rose would try to make me eat out of dirty chicken troughs. And another time, she tried to make me eat dead cockroaches. Now that was one time I rebelled. Of course, I really got a beating. She loved to twist my face, my pudgy, cheeks. I had a bruise all the time. Daddy asked me what did I do and I said I ran into the door. Not to bad a lie for a kid I guess. Except I was a tiny little girl and not just weight wise, but height wise as well. Nobody should have believed that lie. My Daddy seemed to think whatever we said it was brought on by jealousy towards the new mother that he had brought into the house.

She would cook food, something like a whopping big turkey with all the trimmings and put it in the refrigerator and dare us to eat any of it. We got good at avoiding that trap. No matter how hungry we got, we left it alone. Then she would tamper with it herself. In addition, raise a fuss about someone eating the food. Daddy would ask who did it. Well, of course, we all answered, "I don't know". By the time he got to me, he was tired of hearing that answer. So the next order of business was spanking. He always started the questioning with Nancy but the spankings always started with me. He always said, "I'll spank all 3 and that way I know I will get the guilty one" When that didn't get a confession from either of us, she went on to more terrible things. She knew I hated my hair braided because she pulled it so tight I got terrible headaches and my eyes were pulled back so far, I looked Japanese. It was so painful I learned another trick. Leave the house with braids and start taking them out before I got to the bus stop. Another time Rose was on Dot's case for a change. She was ready to go to the bus stop and was eating her breakfast. When Rose asked her if she wanted some gravy, Dot said no, but Rose thought she should eat some. And before any of us could say or do anything, Rose calmly picked up the bowl of gravy and poured it over Dot's head. It ran down Dot's hair, her face and onto her dress. She started to cry. I remember Daddy sitting there not doing a thing for her. I never did know how Dot got to school or even if she went that day. My turn came a few days later. That day Rose decided to have beets for supper. Not just sliced beets but beets as big as softballs. I never did care for them and that day I didn't want any, especially those big ones. Rose said, "You will eat these" I said "no thanks" She said, "you will sit at this table until you do" I said "I will not eat any beets" Guess what? I was sitting there 3 hours later.

Every time Dot and Nancy came through, they each would take a beet outside. Never did know what they did with them. Hope they didn't have to eat them. Then another time Dot decided she wanted some prunes and the box wasn't opened yet. First mistake, opening the box, second mistake, taking 2 lousy prunes out to eat. When Rose got home, the first thing she always did was check her traps. Well, Dot was caught. So Rose made her eat the whole box of prunes. Poor Dot, she spent a lot of time on the toilet. She was so weakened by all that, she spent a day in bed. We thought Rose felt bad after that. Wrong!! She went into El Paso and went on a shopping spree and bought all of us so many new clothes, from the skin out. Hats, shoes, socks, coats, everything to make 3 little girls happy. She lined them up in our closets and let us look at them and think what a great woman she was, and possibly, she might be learning to love 3 little girls.

We 3 went to school the next 2 or 3 days so happy. And when we got home on Friday, our closets were as bare as Mother Hubbard's cupboard. Oh!!! The disappointment. We 3 clung together and cried our eyes out. Then as an added punishment the next morning, she got me up and made me walk to the base of the Sugarloaf Mountain because she thought I was to skinny. She thought it would fatten me up by making me eat more. Can you imagine? What was I suppose to eat? Not anything in the refrigerator. So I did walk about a week. Then my brain kicked in and I thought "this is dumb" So I figured out that I would walk so far that she couldn't see me, sit down and wait for the right amount of time and start walking back. Well guess what? She'd done it again. She had climbed up on our garage, which had a flat roof, and watched me with binoculars!!! OH LORD!!!! Did I catch it that time.

While all this is going on with us, I often wondered where my mother and her family were. But then I remembered how Nancy was sent to Virginia while Daddy was gone for 4 years. Dot and I were left outside in the back yard in the dark while my mother's sister was getting married. Two little girls left out in the dark about 9 p.m. I wasn't going to be out done. I started swinging as high as I could and shouting at the top of my lungs. My grandma Paden came outside and took us into the back porch of her house. She paddled my behind with one of her slippers. I looked at her, saying I was going to tell my Daddy when he got home. She paddled some more and I kept saying I was going to tell my Daddy. She actually worn her slipper out on me. I forgot to tell Daddy for years about that. In fact, I finally told him after I married. All he said was "she was an old witch". He didn't even get mad. Some protection again. It seems the Padens didn't want us and neither did the Lovells. Three little girls lost.

After awhile Daddy decided to go to Washington D.C. This was 1948. I was going into the 6th grade. I was so excited, feeling so grown up and all. The very first day the principal called me into the office. She told me I wasn't allowed to wear dungarees to school. I said I wasn't wearing dungarees. She said I was. When I said no, I wasn't, she asked me what I had on. I stood tall as my short Texas frame would let me, and proudly said "blue jeans" She then told me a young lady doesn't come to school wearing blue jeans. She wears dresses. All I could say was "I don't have any dresses" She said, "You will by tomorrow or don't come back to school". So this little person went off to the new house Daddy had bought for us and had to tell him I needed dresses. I don't know if he even had the money to go shopping, but he did. I always felt like an orphan. It wasn't easy for a man back in those days to be a single parent.

But for a man to raise 3 girls and be ready to tell us girls things must have been a hard job. Today it is accepted as everyday but not back in 1948. Only 3 years after the big war.

I watched other girls and tried to dress something like them. Never really got the job done because we didn't have the money. So I tried to make my own money by babysitting or gathering pop bottles to redeem for 5 cents a bottle or even going around the neighborhood asking the men and women to let me polish their shoes for 10 cents a pair. I'm here to tell you I could put a shine on their shoes that you could see yourself in. Daddy being army for so many years had taught me how to polish shoes and fold a flag. Some of the men in the neighborhood were government employees so their shoes had to pass inspection. Regulation shine. It gave me a little money. Back then, I would baby sit for 3 or 4 kids in a house for a whopping 35 cents an hour. Dot or Nancy wasn't into doing that as much as I was. All the people in our neighborhood saved their bottles for me... the little moneygrubber. And they knew I would stay late but not once did a husband ever think to walk me home. Times were different then. I would go prowling on the weekends, all by myself. I trusted people so much, it's a wonder I wasn't butchered. One good example was a time I went down Ardmore road to the railroad tracks. I did that a lot and cut through the woods to dig flowers. The railroad switch tower was there, so what do I do but climb up into the tower. A total stranger was there working the switches and was kind enough to show a little girl how it worked. Today I could have run into Jack the Ripper. I remember him because he was so nice. I guess I needed attention so badly. I would get it wherever I could. After awhile he sent me on my way with a friendly smile.

Then before I knew it, Daddy was gone again, back to Texas and brought the stepmother from Hell to Maryland. Oh, how I prayed to God and asked him "what had we done to deserve this all over again?" It was happening the same as before. Could our father be so blind? Only this time she had a partner in crime. And it seemed it gave her a new bravado she didn't have before. Crueler than before. Whenever she was ticked off, she would clean out the house. I always went to Sunday school and church every week. In fact, Daddy always yelled at me to get up me up for church but not Dot or Nancy. I tried several churches trying to find my way and was working on my lessons for the Lutheran church. My minister came to my house and Rose promptly sat him down started telling him how bad we were and that we put our soiled sanitary napkins in the refrigerator. Well that embarrassed me so bad I refuse to go back to church and I couldn't face my minister. He finally came and asked me to go back but I couldn't even look at him and just said no.

She wasn't done yet. She was always watching us, waiting her chance. Like back in Texas. That time she thought she had finally gone too far. She accused us of breaking her jewelry. And of course, we hadn't touched it. It was late at night, it must have been very late because I remember a neighbor taking us in after awhile. It started with Rose screaming about her damn jewelry. She kept it up and kept it up. Until Daddy, who was on crutches from a motorcycle wreck, finally got fed up and got a gun and literally chased we three girls all over Logan Heights, yelling "I'll kill you, all of you, I swear to God I'll kill you all" Here we are 3 little girls in ragged pajamas, trying to run in that Texas dirt that has sand burrs that tore at your feet. None of us had put on any shoes. We really thought had he caught us, we would be dead.

None of us stopped running. We really thought if he caught up with us, we'd be dead. The trauma of my Daddy chasing me, saying he would kill me never left my memory. That was the only time anyone helped. It was called "interfering" back in those days. Children were treated as property and what went on behind closed doors was nobody's business. But that time our neighbors took us into their house and we sat there the rest of the night, shivering so hard our teeth rattled.

Well, every time Rose came back to the house, she tried something new. By this time, I was getting some age on me and feeling a bit more brave. I had been taught to respect my elders, but it seemed to me, that all my life, it was a one-way street. I was always beat down on all sides. But expected to act a different way from the adult world. I had ideas of things I wanted to do, but no one encouraged me. When Rose came in for that one last time, I was sitting at the dining room table doing my homework, which I hadn't done earlier that evening. I waited until Daddy went to work, at 11:00 p.m. and got back up to do it. She came in and started her usual stuff. She and her friend. They both promptly started calling Daddy names and I jumped in and told her friend to shut up and to leave our house. She looked at Rose and said, "Are you going to let her talk to me like that?" I said, "She can't stop me, you don't have any right to come into our house and start calling my Dad those filthy names". Rose backed me into a corner of the kitchen and made a motion to grab my face again. So I raised my hand and told him if she even tried it, I would let her have it too. She didn't believe me. She let me have it right across my face. And at the same time, whack, I let her have it across her face as well. She stepped back, looking shocked and screeching like a banshee. "Did you see that?" "Did you see what she did?"

Children were treated as property and what went on behind closed doors was nobody's business.

Every time Rose came back to the house, she tried something new. By this time, I was getting into my early teens. But it seemed to me that all my life it was a one-way street. I was always beat down on all sides. But expected to act a different way from the adult world.

I had ideas of things I wanted to do, but no one to encourage me. When Rose came in for that last time, I was sitting at the dining room table doing homework. I hadn't done it earlier that evening. I waited until Daddy went to work which was 11:00 p.m. and started doing my homework. She came in and started her crap. She and her friend. They both promptly started calling Daddy names and snooping into his things. She looked at Rose and said, "look, he has a lock on this door," I said," he has that on there for a reason, to keep nosey people out of his business" Rose backed me into a corner and made like she was going to do her usual abuse. So I raised my hand and told her if she tried it, it would be the last time she ever hit me. She didn't believe me. . But believe it or not, it was the last time she ever put a hand on me. She stepped back, looking shocked and screeching like a banshee. "Did you see that?" "Did you see what she did?" Her friend said, "Boy, I wouldn't let her get away with that" "the little white trash". Then I told her she had 3 seconds to get out of the house. By that time, Nancy came out of her bedroom and asked what was going on. I said Rose was at it again. She was trying to take everything in the house, like always. So we offered to help her. When she tried to take certain things, we said, "ok that's yours" or "no, that's Daddy's".

Not exactly. It seemed I couldn't do anything to make Dad happy. By this time, I was in High school in Maryland. Bladensburg to be exact. Thinking really grown up. I got involved in some projects, drama class for one. I was always fascinated by plays and acting. I did get into one play, but come play night and my debut, there wasn't anybody in the audience for me. All the other kids had parents, aunts and uncles As usual, one more disappointment. I played basketball but nobody came. I must admit I wasn't the best student in the class, but I got enough grades to get by. I think I really needed glasses. By the time my sophomore year ended, I was really thinking grown up. Not expecting to get married right away or anything, but thought I would get married someday and have 2 baby girls. I had always lavished love on 2 doll babies. I played house and it was always 2 dolls and it was going to be girls.

Boys just didn't figure into my picture .It was going to be girls, period. This was about the time Dad told me to get into the kitchen and learn to cook. I was out walking our dog, Pal. Dot was with me for once and we were walking down Ardmore Rd. when a car came barreling up. I was afraid they were going to run over my dog. I told the two soldiers in the car if they hurt my dog, they would have to answer to my Dad. And he was a government cop. They started laughing. They stayed parked at the side of the road for a while. And we all talked, getting to know each other. Then the soldier doing the driving asked us to get in. This car was what was called the community car at the camp. The driver happened to be Dave, my future husband. So Dot and I piled into the back seat of the car. When the guys got passes, they got to use the car. The back door was tied with a combat bootlace to keep the door closed. To get into the car, you had to climb over the driver. I never knew if this was by design or not.

We went out several times and then Dave was sent to Delaware for that good old word again, maneuvers. He was gone for about a month. I wrote him everyday. And when he came back to camp, I was ready to see him by then. After we had gone together for about 2 months, he asked me to marry him. I said, "Yes I would marry him, but I was sure Dad wouldn't let us get married". After all, I was only 16 years old. Dave said, "If your Dad won't let us get married, I will make you pregnant, and then he will have to let us marry". I said, "Oh no you won't. Nobody will ever say I was like my mother". That's the one thing I held very close to my heart. No one would ever say "Like mother like daughter". In the long run, I guess Dad thought if he let us marry, it would be one less problem for him. So he signed the papers and Dave and I set our time to get married. Well guess what? My Dad wouldn't even go to our simple little wedding. He was very busy washing his car. Tells you which was more important to him. One more disappointment.

After 6 months Dave and I found out I was pregnant. Two months before that, Dad had gone back to Texas and gotten married to a woman named Myrtle. And whammo, she was pregnant as well. She was 39 years old, but acted like she was 16. When my time came to deliver my first daughter, my Dad didn't have the decency to act glad about his first granddaughter. Just another "split-tail" as he called us all of the female gender. From that time on, there was full-blown competition between all of us. My sisters couldn't do anything acceptable. And God knows I wasn't a good mother in their eyes. Myrtle had a son and a daughter from her first marriage. Dad only thought of them as his. But not us. The same old stuff. Myrtle always felt we were a threat. Really don't know why. I was already married.

Granite, Dave and I didn't have a lot of money and the Army pay didn't reach the end of the month.

But we always thought family was there to help each other. When I think back on it, even though I was married, Dad still thought he had control of me. Even after Dave and I were married, Dad beat the holy hell out of me. He said I had back-talked him. I didn't. I was just trying to explain why Dave and I were out so late the night before. We had gone to Richmond so I could introduce him to my cousins. I asked him what harm had been done anyway? I was married to him. And that's all she wrote. He hauled off and backhanded me right in the face with a Mason's ring. Talk about a black eye. I locked myself in the bathroom while Dad ranted and raved outside .Dave was outside working on our old Hudson coupe. When Dave finally came into the house and saw what Dad had done, he was ready to go and beat the tar out of my Dad. But Dad beat Dave to the punch by saying, "I know I shouldn't have hit her." Whoopee! That didn't help my face. I told Dave I was moving out. It was a Sunday and Dave said, "Where are we going?" I said I don't care where we went as long as it's out of here. So we lived 3 days in our little Hudson coupe. We had to park outside the camp while Dave did his duty. I sat in the car. The men from the camp brought out K and C rations and a lot of fruit for me to eat. God love 'em. Enough fruit to fill the space under the back seat We finally found an apartment in Bladensburg on Buchanan St. We stayed there for a few months. I had a lot of fun being Mrs. Gartrell. And then we moved to Kennedy St. in Hyattsville, to wait for the baby to be born.

I wasn't doing good during this time but never told Dad. I did my monthly checkups at Walter Reed Army hospital. And then it was time to go and become a mother. She was a beautiful baby girl, just like I said I would have. My Dad was such a cheap skate, he didn't hardly recognize her as his granddaughter.... Not even a small gift. But what else is new???

Yep, you guessed it... another girl. But Myrtle was so afraid of my child, she wouldn't have anything to do with us. She went out of her way to spread such gossip and hurtful things. I only tolerated her because Dad picked her as his mate. By this time, Dave was discharged out of the Army. So off to Ohio we went with a 3 week old baby in tow. Dot and her future husband went with us. None of us knew we would practically starve because the guys couldn't get a job.

We learned to do a lot of hunting for rabbits just to have rabbit and gravy bread to eat. But it was something to eat. The baby had her food and milk because we saved Dave's mustering out pay from the Army so she could have hers. We used real cloth diapers back then, so that wasn't a problem. Except they froze solid before I could get them on the clothesline. I felt good being a wife and mother. Even though there were times I was so scared. I didn't know what was going to happen next. I always felt like a survivor. Maybe my early years helped me to be so. I can jump into a situation and help and feel good when it's over. Maybe I've been lucky when it comes to being able to go on with a different type of attitude. Nancy and Dot both suffered from different personalities than me. My poor sister Dot, let all those early years eat at her all those years, like a cancer.

The older she got, the worse it became for her. She always thought we didn't love her. Many a time she attacked me. Nothing important. Just one word led to another and before we knew it, we were at each other's throats. I was thrown out of her house so many times; I can't begin to tell you just how many times it was. Didn't matter how far we had come. If the mood struck her, out we would go. And Nancy, she did the opposite. She became a hermit. Totally stays away from all of us. If I want to talk to her, I have to do the calling. Nancy married and had 3 sons. They live back in Norton, VA where my Dad's family lived and worked as coal miners.

She always says she will write or call but she never does. Dot died when she was only 58 yrs. She didn't have to die so young, but you know what? I think she just gave up. She finally got fed up with the crap. She always thought God was picking on her. But I kept telling her we were there to. I know how hurt she was. When our Mother died, Dot broke down and cried saying," she died never telling me she loved me." I tried to tell her our mother never told me she loved me either, so don't feel bad. But when your own mother doesn't want you, who will?

After Ohio, we headed out to Tennessee. That lasted for 2 years. That's about how long I could stomach Myrtle. Then we hitched our wagon to another star and headed west. We lived in Rangely, Colorado for about 2 more years. Then Dave got wind of Nevada. About all the money to be made in the mine work. We got everything ready and came to Nevada. We didn't have our mobile home in Nevada for about 3 months, so we lived in a truck camper. Oh, I nearly went crazy. Did a lot of crocheting. I'll tell you, when I saw the top of our mobile home coming into Gopher Gulch, I was one happy camper. This was the Victoria mine. I was the only Protestant out there I think. Everyone else was LDS. As long as I said yes, all went well. But the first time I disagreed, it hit the fan.

As a kid trying to grow up in El Paso, it was one of those things of not knowing for a while that you are so different from all the other, more well off kids. My life evolved around Logan Heights, Dyer Street and Winkler school. We actually lived on Kemp St. I was a tomboy, always trying to be the boy. My Dad wanted a boy so bad. I tried to walk like him and thought because everyone said I looked just like him, I would be a boy for him. When in all reality, I turned out to be a very nice girl. HA!

I would go off to the Crawford Theater in downtown El Paso, for the weekly serials of Flash Gordon, Gene Autry, Roy Rogers or Rocket Man. I would even go see the most scariest movies of the Mummy. And I'm here to tell you, they scared the socks off of me. I always knew when the scene showed the moon with clouds going over the moon, it meant the Mummy was going to walk. And I also knew the music. So while all this was going on, I had my eyes closed so tight you couldn't have pried them open with a crow bar. When all the good stuff was over, I went back to watching the movie. Once, during one of the Mummy movies, I don't remember which one it was, I got scared so bad, I took off up the rows looking for my Dad. It was one of the few times he went. In the dark of the theater, all I could see was the shiny, Army brass buttons on the uniform. I took a running leap and dived right into the arms of the uniform. The kind man patted me on the back and said, "It's ok honey, it will be alright in just a few minutes." I thought, "This doesn't sound like Daddy". I looked up and right into the soldier's face. I was right, it wasn't Daddy. It was a nice soldier from Fort Bliss, in town on a pass. I'm sure he would have preferred a bigger girl sitting on his lap.

I was forever picking up strays. Never thinking they might belong to anyone. The school was a good 2 miles from home. I was supposed to ride the school bus home. But I always was on an adventure. This one day I saw the most beautiful dog. It was a full-grown Great Dane. Well, I couldn't see this poor animal running loose, could I? So I got hold of his collar and proceeded to walk home. I didn't have a barn for this horse of a dog, so I took him in our house. When Dad got home, the dog in the meantime had eaten everything off the table, he asked, "where did this horse come from?" I told him it followed me home...Original huh? He said, "Well, tomorrow it will follow you right back". I said they wouldn't let me on the bus with him. His answer was," it didn't ride the bus here." Needless to say, I had to get up very early the next morning and walk him back to the school. Now when I think of it, I'm sure the owners were very worried about their pet. But he did eat well.

Another time, again while walking home from school, I saw this little chipmunk in the doorway of a bowling alley. I looked around to find something to put him in. I did find a small coffee can and finally got the little critter inside the can. The first thing I did was reach in and grab my new pet. Well, the first thing my new pet did was put the chomp on my little finger. For such a little critter, it sure had a set of big teeth. I slung my hand as hard as I could, and he finally let go and hit the ground running. That was the last I ever saw of him. Didn't know I could have got rabies and never did tell Dad.

I was always getting hurt with rusty nails etc., and wouldn't tell Dad because he would never give you any sympathy, only wrath .When it would get infected, and to the point of no return, I would be forced to tell him or he would see me hobbling around and he would start cussing,

He would get out a bucket for hot water and salt to make me soak whatever part was affected. Of course, it did make it feel better.

In downtown El Paso, there was an alligator pond. I would sit and wait for one of those big gators to move. Open an eye even. After some time, I came to believe they weren't real. They never did move, not even once. I know now they were real. It was their nature to just lie in the sun and be quiet, and sleep, sleep, and sleep some more. I am really surprised I didn't climb over the wall and go visit them one on one. I would sit there for hours trying not to go home. Or I would be found in the movies. I knew if I went to the house, I would be Rose's victim again. Some terrible punishment or torture she would think up. We three girls suffered all this done to us because we thought our Dad didn't know. But I know now, he did know. We thought we were protecting him and his feelings. What a joke!

Parents are supposed to protect their children. After my mother did what she did to all of us, I realize the only reason my Dad took us was to get revenge against my mother. But the ironic thing is she didn't want us so it backfired on him. In 1945, when they got divorced, men weren't given custody solely. But he always told us he got the custody of us. He would ask once in a while if I wanted to go to her. If I did, he would see that I got to her. But he knew me well enough to know I wouldn't go to her. I should have wondered how he was going to do this, since he had sole custody. He kidnapped us girls and ran clear across the United States to Washington D.C. I don't think he had to run that far because she had already forgotten us girls and gone on with her life. She had married a man named Loomis and had 4 more daughters. Years later, I found some of my relatives on the Paden side.

My uncles told me they had asked where we were for years, and she always said she didn't know. She always knew because she would write once in a while. Just to me and nobody else. Then in her old age, she got sick. The daughters she had with Loomis after us would call me and tell me she was sick in Salt Lake City. I went a couple of times. They said she was in a bad way but when ever we got there, she was always up and around .It was like they cried "WOLF" to many times. She was very bad off financially. She didn't have much. But the girls thought me and my husband should put out money to her. I said "no". I told them "you had a mother during your growing up years, so now you be there for her now that she is dying". When she did die, my oldest daughter, Roberta, went to the funeral with me in Kearns, Utah. It closed that chapter of my life. This woman was so selfish she chose to leave 3 little girls on Christmas Eve. I was sent to a church Christmas party. I can even tell you what the little gift was. A glass doll bottle with a rubber nipple, a rubber water bottle and a diaper, all as a layette, I guess. But, to this day, I can't remember a single Christmas before that one. I even asked Dad did we ever celebrate Christmas before she left and he said yes. He said we always had big

Christmases But I can't remember any of them. Strange, it must be because she chose to leave on that holiday. I have always had a hard time with the blues after Thanksgiving. And, of course, the Padens never gave us anything, not even love. And it's free.

After Dad took us to D.C., I was on my own again to learn as best I could. I made friends mainly because of my out going ways I guess. The kids in Landover Hills were pretty good kids.

A better class of people than I was used to. These kids treated me very nice. In fact, after all these years, I still keep in touch with one of the very first girls I met in school.

I went to school everyday but to tell the truth, I don't think Dad knew except on report card day. He scratched his name on it and handed it back. Never a comment on the bad grades. I got through 6th and 7th ok. And then I found D.C. and all the wonderful buildings in our Nation's capital. I would play hooky every chance I got. I would ride the transit bus into D.C. and go from building to building. I even went into the capital building, went up into the gallery and sat there watching our politicians doing their jobs. And some were catching up on their sleep. I would go to all the important buildings more than once. I felt like I belonged there. I would skip school a lot but you know what? I wasn't even missed. I would forge Dad's signature on some kind of excuse and they accepted it. I wandered around the streets alone. A little kid. Can you imagine and nobody even stopped me and asked me what I was doing there or where were my parents.

I hated the things we had to put up with at house. Rose would find reasons to un-do everything we tried to do. If I wanted to ride a bike, or play dolls, she would start with the punishments. Or rather, the torments. No matter what time of the day or night. I don't know when she slept. Because she would stay up all night with us and when she got worn out from all that beating, she would rest for awhile and start all over again. She must have done her sleeping during the days while we were at school. We were black and blue with bruises but our teachers or preachers never asked. My main job, as the smallest, was to take out the trash at night. I would lie down and before you knew it, I was asleep. Nancy and Dot would wake me up about 9:00 p.m. and tell me to take it out or suffer the effects. I would get up, groggy with sleep and get the trash and wander down the alley to a neighbor's can and dump it in.

Then I would run like a scalded dog back to our house. Never did I figure out why I chose the neighbor's can. Except, in my mind, the Mummy was going to walk by ours.

It was so bad it was bound to affect our young minds. And because Dot was the proverbial middle child, I really think it was a force so strong she couldn't come to grips with it. And as the years went on, it grew worse. She married and had 4 children, 3 girls and 1 boy. The first daughter, Vickie Lynn, only lived 1 ½ days and that was another strike against Dot. She started to lose what faith she had, screaming there was no God. I thought she was getting better after she got pregnant with her second child, Leona. Then she had a third daughter, Holly and finally a son, Jeff. She thought, foolishly, that would make Dad love her more because it was a boy. It didn't.

Then Nancy had 3 boys in a row and things did not change there either. We all settled into a routine. Living our lives and trying to forget the cruelty of our youth, Dave and I went on with our lives and 2 years after out first daughter was born, I had our second daughter. Just like my plans. The first one we named Roberta, which we shortened to Berta, and the second one we named Peggy. Berta was our little lady and Peggy was my little Tomboy and a rough neck. I would spend hours getting Peggy ready to go somewhere and she would promptly go outside and fall in a mud puddle. Berta couldn't even stand water dribbled on her dresses. Or she would want a fresh dress on. Not having a mother to set examples, I was doing mainly by trial and error. And since babies don't come with manuals, I did the best I could. We had some serious accidents, and sicknesses, but Thank God, nothing to try us to the point of collapse. We thought we were the masters of our fate.

We started out in Texas as kids, went to Maryland and started back west without realizing it. But when Dad brought Rose to Maryland, after all we had gone through it was just too much. Nancy withdrew more and more. Dot had such a hair trigger temper and I did as well, anything could happen and usually did, between Dot and I. Maybe because she and I were so much alike, I would say the wrong thing or she did and the war was on. She would grab a fist full of my hair and swing me around. I could take that because I was very tough headed but she wasn't at all. When I would get my chance, I would get my fingers in her hair and pull, thinking she would let go. That's what I get for thinking...Not a good plan. It just set her off more. She would start screaming she was going to kill me, and for me to let go of her hair. And believe me, she really tried. Being bigger than me, she would finally get me down on the floor. Ouch!

She would sit on me and do her best to suffocate me with a pillow she grabbed off the sofa. All the while saying, "I'll kill you and I hate you" through clenched teeth. Another time she grabbed a pair of scissors and was chasing me through the house like Norman Bates trying to stab me. Nancy stepped in and tried to get the scissors away from Dot. And Dot plunged the blades into Nancy's upper arm. I think by that time Nancy made up her mind not to help Gladys anymore. I was on my own. All Nancy would say was "you better watch out and be quiet." While she tried to get the bleeding to stop. It was in the upper part of her arm, so Dad never knew Dot had tried to murder us. These battles never occurred when Dad was home. Mainly because we feared his wrath .He always worked at night and tried sleeping during the days. If a salesman came to the door while we were at school, we always knew it when we got home. Mainly because his mood was so bad. He always took it out on us. We had an old dog I found. He was an English bird dog.

A stray. Totally eat up with ticks and fleas. Dirty and grungy. And he was so hungry. I begged Dad to let me keep him. He did give in and I promised to take care of him. It took me forever to clean him up. I named him "Silver". He was already old when I found him. And I didn't know he was deaf as well. He would get scared of being alone. The minute he thought he was by himself, he would start barking. I also got blamed for that too. I learned to sit with the dog and touch him for hours just so he thought he wasn't alone and Dad could sleep. He was a lovable dog and always acted grateful for us taking him in. We had him for many years even though he was old, and he died on a hot summer day, on a weekend. He must have known he was dying and tried to wander off to die alone. He didn't make it, he dropped in the sun. Well, guess who got the blame for Silver dying? You got it! Me! Dad kept saying I wasn't watching him like I should. Other than toting him around in my hip pocket, I don't know what else I could have done. I cried for that old dog. He was a friend with un-conditional love. I'm sure he knew he was loved.

It seemed that Dad always got tangled up with women who didn't like kids or dogs. Especially these kids or dogs. I finally got tired of the "holier than thou" attitude and said out loud "you know, people who don't like dogs aren't very nice people" And the Bible says God will take care of any body who takes care of their beasts. At least one, Myrtle, tried to fake it after that. Rose didn't even try.

Even after coming to Maryland, Rose was her usual self. She did her level best to make us hate her. Which wasn't that hard to do. I think by this time, we had become hardened to everything around us. More defensive. Whenever Rose decided to take a ball bat, figuratively speaking, we got out of the way.

She managed to get people to believe her and get them on her side. And in Maryland, she pulled the same old stuff with the beautiful clothes. I remember it was Easter weekend. We got the whole works, and as soon as Easter Monday rolled around, gone were the clothes. Never knew what she did with them. She may have taken them back to the store and gotten her money back. And then again, she may have felt big-hearted and gave them to Goodwill. It makes me happy to think some little girl might have gotten new clothes. I would be invited, by the kids in Maryland, to their homes and found out, not all people lived like we did. The parents were so loving and caring to their kids. I was included in that picture and I came to realize people, some people, were very nice. I didn't have to flinch when an adult walked by. I learned to love people and trust them. I think I was finding out, without knowing it, I had road to follow. I was growing up. I had to be strong… I was strong

I remember when I was in the 8th grade, I wrote a short story about being born and living in Texas. I was still very homesick for my home state. I put it all on a piece of paper. I got my nerve up and asked my teacher if I could read it to the class. He read it and said yes. So I got real brave and read it to the class .and .them in stitches. My teacher was laughing as hard as the class. He told me to keep writing and always follow what I wanted to do. That was the last thing I tried to write for years. He gave me a double "A" for a grade. Pretty good huh?

Somewhere along the way, I got interested in Civil War history. I was so interested in it that it seemed to come naturally. And later, when my daughters were in the 5th grade, at different times, they both had the same teacher, who was a southerner. Her name was Davis.

I've often thought she was married to a relative of Jefferson Davis because she refused to teach that chapter of the Civil War. She knew I had civil war songs and material. So she asked me if I would be interested in doing something with the kids. We had a ball. Mrs. Davis is still waiting for the south to rise again.

While I was busy with my family, I got a call from Maryland telling me Dad in the hospital, so we scraped some money together and Dot and I took off for Maryland. I never understood how we could be so mistreated and jump to his aid. But we always did. We stayed for about a month and he got better. Whenever he got sick, I always sent flowers and prayed he would do better.

The girls were growing and doing different things and we tried to do them with them. They went to church every Sunday and to Bible school in the summers. They asked me to be Room mother for them when they were in the 5th grades. Which I did. Then came scouting. To be fair with the girls I refused to be their leader. I wanted them to be treated fairly and afraid I would lean to far one way or the other. Either give too much or take too much. So I wanted each to have their own leader. That way, they would have a chance to learn and do well on their own merits. Not because I was biased. We had such fun doing badges for their sashes. I had my own troop to lead and it was so much fun, showing the girls how to do things.

Then we got this wild idea... Let's move back to Maryland! I mean how dumb can you be? We thought wages would be bigger and maybe have benefits. So we packed everything we owned into a pickup truck and off we went. Dave had no trouble getting a job. Right off, he was working in a garage. We found this dumpy little house in Lanham, Md. It was practically across the street from Dad and Myrtle. Foolish move. Foolish, foolish move.

Dot and her husband, Mac, lived several miles away in Bowie. The headaches and heartaches started all over again. Take Christmas that year. I spent hours and hours decorating Dad's house with the tree and painted scenes on each panel of a big window in the front of the house. There were 10 panels. When Dad got home, he asked who painted the window? I said I did. He said he never knew I could draw. I told him I had been drawing for years. I always took art classes in school. And we had planned for all of us, as family, to be together for Christmas. We managed to find a big tree and got it decorated. And for some reason, and I have never understood, Dot got upset and before I knew it, we were all yelling at each other. Hurling insults. She refused to come for Christmas. Needless to say, it wasn't a happy day. Everyone darting glances at each other and it seemed every bit of food stuck in my throat. None of us wanted to exchange gifts but for the sake of the kids, we did. It seemed in my mind Christmas just wasn't my holiday. It wasn't long after that, we decided to go back to Ohio. And try our luck again. We didn't do much better in wages, but at least it was more peaceful. And after awhile you start to let your guard down again. And think that because you are 500 miles away from them, everything is going along smoothly. It wasn't. We found out the gossips had been at it all along. From family members, we were told how we were being blamed for a whole bunch of stuff. From stealing to carrying tales. We were blamed because we were so far away and wouldn't hear about it for along time. And Myrtle thought by the time we heard about it, I wouldn't say anything to correct it. But I did. I always did. But all it did was put me on top of the list again. Trouble making Gladys. The son and daughter of Myrtle were the "I don't do anything" twins. If a story got around that so and so said this or that, nobody ever knew anything about it.

They could lie with a straight face. No digging the toe in the dirt, no rolling the eyes toward the ceiling, no nothing. We were told by her son, "this is our house now, why don't you leave?" "You are not wanted here." After awhile, because he didn't get his way, he left and went back to Texas and lived with his Dad for some time. That didn't work for him either so he came back to his mother. And when he did, he slandered his own mother so bad it nearly broke her heart. What goes around comes around.

Dot would tell me she was so jealous of Linda, Dad and Myrtle's new little girl. I wouldn't be jealous of her because she was more lucky than us in a way, and in another, she wasn't. I saw her get tons of toys and clothes, but nothing in the way of LOVE. Both parents worked and she was left to fend for herself. They never knew what she was doing, and believe me, she was always into no good. She got into all kinds of trouble in school and then got messed up with drugs. She got married to a drugged out guy who threatened to beat me with a garden hose. He thought he could because he was used to beating Linda. I don't think it would have worked with me. I may have ended up on the floor, but I'm sure I would have gotten a few licks in. He was the kind of guy who was brave as long as he was beating up women.

We were all trying to grow up I guess. The girls loved spending time with their cousins and we would have little birthday parties together or we would go to the little town they lived in and go trick or treating together. We would go to Dot's house for a few hours on Christmas and have a good time, if we were lucky. Then Dave and I would load the girls and toys in our car and head off for Dayton and Dave's Mom's house so we could spend a few hours with her. It seemed like that's what we always did.

Finally, Mom said, "why don't all of you come to my house and you don't have to be on the road all day?" We agreed to that. And it worked for awhile.

By this time, Dad had retired from the government and Myrtle from her job. They decided to move back to Texas. But somehow, they got side tracked and ended up in Tennessee. They got hired to run a tourist court. Lots of rooms and cabins and a swimming pool. They invited us down and showed us a house they were trying to buy. They asked us if we wanted to rent it from them. It sounded good. So we went back to Ohio and loaded up our stuff. Another bad decision. That is the one time where Myrtle and I came to verbal blows. One time she wanted Dad to kill a chicken for supper and he said NO, he wasn't going to kill any chicken. He walked out of the house and went to do whatever he was going to do. The minute he got out of earshot, she cut loose, calling him all kinds of wimp, and a few other choice names. I jumped in and said, "If you want to call him names, do it to his face". She told me to shut up, and I said no, and on and on. Both of us getting louder and louder. Finally, who walks in the door but Dad. He said, "What the hell is going on?" and before I could say a word, she acted like the offended one. In her words "your daughter is being abusive and I don't like it. I want her out of here." I said "don't worry, I'm out of here."" But ask your loving wife why I was disrespectful." I sure she didn't tell him.

Nancy and her family stayed in Maryland. I didn't know it for years that Dad had asked her for money. So she and her husband sold their house and loaned him the money. They bought a doublewide home and Dad was to pay them back. He used the money to re-model the house for Myrtle in Texas.

I remember when I was going with a guy I thought was really great. He was in his early 20's and I was a very young teenager. I suppose, legally, he would have been under the jail instead of in it, if he would have been caught. He was too old for me but I was very flattered by his grown up attention. Then all of a sudden, I decided I didn't want him around anymore. I kept working it around until Dot was going with him. They spent some time together for quite some time. Then, for reasons unknown to any of us, he dropped her. She ranted and raved around the house for some time. One day, while Dad was in town, she came out of the bedroom and said "I did it" and I said, "What did you do?" She said, "I took all those pills." I had no idea what pills she was talking about. I went into the bedroom and on the nightstand was the remains of a glass of water and a few pills scattered on the top of the stand. Also was an empty pitcher there. I asked her how many she had taken but she refused to tell me or Nancy. She was crying and walking back and forth in the living room, wringing her hands and saying things that didn't make sense to me. About that time, Dad drove up and I ran outside and told him. Dot was screaming that Dad was going to kill her for it. I thought it a little ironic that she worried about being killed after taking pills to die. Dad went charging in the front door and Dot went out the back. He told me to go after her. All the while, I was begging her to come back home, and her saying no. I chased her about 4 or 5 blocks, with the neighbors watching, I finally caught up to her. I don't know if it was because she was tired, or if she really wanted me to catch her.

Maybe by that time, she was getting second thoughts about living. Maybe she didn't want to die after all! Anyway, Dad drove up with the car and she calmly got in. He dropped me off at the house and he took her to the hospital. They were gone a long time. Nancy and I sat in the living room and didn't say much.

Finally, he came home. Dot went straight to her room. I went in to see how she was, and she just looked at me and said, "Boy, that doctor was good looking." And she was very mad because he had asked her if she was pregnant. I guess that is standard procedure when girls try to commit suicide. Dad did say that my chasing her for all those blocks had caused her to sweat and that had helped save her life. Whatever did it, I was glad she was still with us.

It was incidents like that, that made me think it was normal, everyday living. One time Dad was whipping the daylights out of us. Don't remember why, just that he was. And the doorbell rang. Low and behold, there were the cops. I guess the neighbors thought that murder was being committed in our house. I do remember it was something Rose was in on. The cops said there had been a complaint made and did a bit of questioning. Since none of us was bleeding and they couldn't see bruises, they said they would leave. We asked if there were any laws against him beating us. They said no. He was our parent and could do anything he wanted, within reason. And they were gone. This was about 1949 or 1950. Things just weren't working out for Rose. We were all still alive and still there.

Always, when Dad left for work at night, he always made sure the front door was locked. Dot and Nancy had a bedroom and lucky me, I slept on the couch in the living room. There were several things that happened that made me wonder. One morning I woke up, very groggy and with a splitting headache. This was before Dad got home. The front door was opened about 2 feet. And there was gas in the house because the furnace had gone out. It had never happened before. If a few more hours had passed, maybe we would have died. Can't prove anything but I have always thought it strange.

Maybe she wanted us out of the family so she could have Dad all to herself. It wasn't because of his money...He didn't have any.

Most people go about their daily lives and never give a thought to what is happening to the innocents of this world. It is such a helpless feeling for children to have to suffer the rampages of adults. As I grew, I always felt drawn to children. I guess that's why I babysat at a very early age. And when I started going with Dave, I knew I wanted to be a wife and a mother. And, for the most part, I have always been pretty happy. I have always been proud of my girls as they grew. I never told them the kind of life we had because I didn't want them not to love their grandfather. As they got bigger, they saw for themselves that he didn't show them any love or affection. And everything went to Linda. Of course, she was their daughter, but my children didn't understand the separation of the two. And as Linda got older, she had a nasty habit of lording it over the rest of us .A better than thou attitude. It was life was repeating itself. Then I could see Myrtle was undermining us more. Always worried about how much Dad leaned in our direction. If it looked like he starting to be considerate or understanding, look out. When Dave and I first got married, we asked Dad to co-sign on a car note for us so we would have a car to get around in. When we moved to Ohio, and

Dave couldn't get a job right off, I asked Dad to pay a payment for us, which was $22.16. He did and as soon as we got money, we paid him back. We didn't want his credit messed up for that payment. We never heard the last of that for the rest of Myrtle's life. And she lived for 38 years with Dad. But her kids could ask for thousands and get it. Some of it never paid back. We three stood on our feet and did without but it made us better for it. Not one of us did drugs or none of us HAD to get married. We have all been married only once.

We all settled in to raise our families. Things didn't always go as smooth as we would have liked. But we did it as best as we could. I was married 10 years before Nancy got married. It was only about 2 years after I got married that Dot tied the knot with Mac. I remember once she got so mad at Mac, her fiancée, she took the ring off her finger and threw it as far she could. I couldn't see the ring being left in the weeds, so I am out there on my hands and knees looking for it. I finally found it. I gave it back to Dot and she wore it for years and finally put it away and wore only her wedding band. But I think our Lovell temper was our worst enemy. Dot and I would explode immediately, but Nancy would take forever to finally let loose. And when she did, everyone within 100 ft. had better get out of her way. It was like a volcano. It covered a wide area. But it seemed she never got over it either. No different than Dot or I.

I am sorry to say, I wasn't around Nancy's boys as they were growing up. And now they are grown men. I don't know their likes or dislikes. Or what they are interested in. They all live in Virginia. Doing whatever it is they do. But as I am getting older, I miss her. And I miss Dot too. The last time I saw Nancy was at Dot's funeral. A long time ago. The state of Virginia is such a long way from Nevada. And we are both getting older, fast.

Then came the time Nancy decided she was ready to be married. So she and her chosen one went to Virginia to tie the knot. We didn't know she had gotten married until about 2 or 3 months after the event. She was telling all about her wedding night and how things went. Remember now, I said I was married 10 years before her. She went on and on telling how she and her husband were virgins and all. I was laughing so hard tears were running down my face. All of a sudden, she looks at me and says "Huh! This married stuff ain't all it's cracked up to be, is it?" I'm here to tell you, I nearly died laughing so hard. But somewhere along the line, they must have figured it out, because they had 3 fine boys. They eventually moved back to Virginia. Back to the coal mining country where my family lived for so many years, and settled in to make their life. She hadn't come out of there for over 10 years now. The last time was when Dot died and she came to Ohio for Dot's funeral. I guess she will stay there the rest of her life.

While these memories come flooding through my mind, another time comes rushing in. This was a Christmas time while we were still in El Paso. Nancy and Dot talked me into sliding under the garage door and go inside and scout out what was in there. I being the smallest and the hole was just big enough for a dumb little girl to go in. Well, I did go in on my back and stood up and turned around and what did I see? A whole big, wonderful, world of toys. Three of everything. Three dolls, three sets of dishes, three Christmas stockings etc. Well, oh boy! That was the time Gladys found out there wasn't a Santa Claus. There was only 2 bicycles, and one pair of roller skates. The girls asked me what I was seeing. I told them they wouldn't believe it. Of course, come Christmas morning, the doll I picked for me went to Nancy and both the girls got the bikes. I got the roller skates. Whoopie!

I had asked for the bike that year, but because I was the youngest, they thought I shouldn't have one. Neither of the girls rode the bikes much and every time I asked to ride one, they, mostly Dot, would charge me rent. Plus, I had to get a 26-inch bike up out of the basement by myself. The top of those stairs seems a long way up. By the time I did get the bike upstairs, I was worn out... I often wonder why I thought it was worth it. Then after I was done riding, I had to put the bike back down in the basement. I was a rule of Dad's. Couldn't leave them outside. Who wanted to ride after all that. Me! But after going through all that, off I'd go. If they decided not to let me ride one of the bikes, I would go to a strip of sidewalk that was the only cement in all of Logan Heights. And I learned to skate. I hated to fall so badly, I made sure I would stay up on my feet .At the end of those precious 30 ft. of cement was a drop off into a pretty good hole. The sidewalk used to have an awning over it but all that was left was a metal pole at the end. When I came to the end of the cement, I would grab the pole and swing around until my feet came back to the cement and I would continue skating. So, I guess I can say not getting a bike was a blessing in disguise. I learned to skate and ride a bike all at the same time. I also learned you have to pay for what you want. When we moved to Maryland, part of our school program was you could either go bowling or skating every Wed. afternoon. I chose skating because I could do it so well. I always looked forward to those afternoons. By that time, Dad bought all 3 of us rink skates. Again, mine were the only ones used. I had my skates until my girls were in scouts and they were working on their skating badges. We leaders took all the troops into Hamilton and did our skating for 4 hours. Peggy came over to me and said, "Gosh Mom, I didn't know you could skate. You're good" How sweet! I did what I always did, skated on my feet so I wouldn't fall down.

The girls did get their badges for their sashes. And I got to sew them on. I guess the early years did teach me the things I needed to know for the future.

When my Dad went over seas, my mother went to Fort Bliss and started working at the PX, (Post Exchange). She worked there at night and she worked at the post movie theater in the refreshment concession. She had to work until the last movie ended and then she had to clean everything for the next day. It would be so late; I would get sleepy and would crawl up on the old cola cooler, the type with 2 sliding doors on the top, and go to sleep until she was done. Many a time her then boyfriend would pick me up and carry me to the bus stop. I can still feel the brass pins cutting into my face from his uniform. The conversation went something like this, "I'll ride the bus on out to your house and carry her inside for you because she is too heavy for you." And that's what he did. But he forgot to go back to Fort Bliss. Nancy said I wasn't old enough to know what was happening. I did understand and I did understand that a strange man was sleeping in my Daddy's bed. The next morning I could hear him getting dressed to go back to camp. And maybe I didn't understand it all, I was only about 5 years old, but I knew it wasn't right so I went outside and play with the three dogs we had. Trixie, Pudgy, and Beausham. It seemed I learned early to turn to my dogs for solace. Or I would go down the alley and play with the neighbor boys. They were typical boys, always playing pranks on each other. There were 3 of them and the youngest one was the butt of jokes. There was a time when the 2 oldest boys got the youngest one down and decided his butt should be bright blue. I mean it was glossy blue paint. Then they took him, naked as a jaybird up on a rock wall that surrounded their yard, and did a stage type play to show him off to the neighbors.

I guess it was funny to most of us, but poor little Wade, it took his mother weeks to scrub it off. We kids were always getting into trouble. I being the only girl in the group, Had to work hard to beat the boys. Once, when I was just barely learning to ride the bike, we decided to have a race. So I got ready to fly on that 26-inch bike. I was going as fast as I could, but I could see the main street coming up fast. I forgot where the brakes were. Not good... I turned the handlebars so I headed out into the desert. Big Mistake! All of a sudden, I was down, going through cactus on both sides of me. When I finally stopped, I looked like a pincushion. Nancy came, carried me home and started pulling out thorns. One consolation, I was winning. But hurt like a son-of-a-gun.

There was a time when I was at the base movie theater and it was summer. So I was at the show barefooted. During intermission, I was in the ladies room getting ready to go back to my seat. I was on one side of the door and someone came in at the same time, catching my big toe under the door. OHHHHHH! It hurt. By the next morning my toe was swelled so big and the base of the nail was turning black. It continued to blacken until the whole nail was involved. The pressure built up to the point that I couldn't do anything but cry. Just writing this brings it all back. My Mother should have taken me to the doctor and maybe they could have done something to lessen the pain. But she and her boyfriend just kept telling me to be quiet. It was so bad I couldn't walk to the bathroom. So her boyfriend would carry me. But the minute he put my legs hanging down below my waist, I could feel my heart beating and throbbing in my toe and cry out in pain. No one offered any relief. Not even an aspirin. It finally started to heal, and the nail started to raise up and was being held by only a tiny piece of nail.

I was at church hobbling around on the back of my heel, going to Vacation Bible School. Trying not to look obvious, when one of the little girls turned around and hit my foot. Off came the nail and it was on its way to complete healing. When I was a very little girl, my mother would send me to the store to buy her cigarettes and I was supposed to go right back home. By the time I did get home, that pack of cigarettes didn't look to good. I would throw them as high as I could and use a stick to whack them, like a baseball. My guess is, probably half were broken in half. Well, it wasn't a good idea to smoke anyway...I didn't know it back then though...

She liked to play cards and some of her friends would meet at our house and they all ate candy and drank coca colas. Of course, we were sent out into the yard like the poor relations.

Then came the time for Daddy to come home. I can see the

inside of our house so vividly. A knock at the door and me running to open it. Who was standing there but Santa Claus. I started backing up into the dining room. He had been sent to help make our Christmas better. He finally got me talked into trusting him and he gave each of us gifts when somebody else came in the door. It was a stranger to me. A very skinny, shaggy haired man, wearing a soldier's uniform. He kept saying, "It's me, Daddy." But he didn't look like the man I remembered. He didn't look like the picture of the soldier we took to the theater and had shown on the screen along with other service men. This man was battle worn and crying. He had already had a run in with my mother. When he saw us scruffy kids, it was heartbreaking to him. He had already threatened our mother and said he was going to kill her if she hadn't decided the better part of valor was cowardice. She and her boyfriend became very scarce. He had been wounded in the Islands in the Pacific and he still wasn't well. He needed more time in the hospital.

Every time a plane flew over, either landing or taking off from Biggs air base, Daddy would dive under the nearest cover. I've seen him under chairs, or the dining room table or even a plant. You don't get over that trauma of war so easy. Of course, we didn't know it all. Up until he died I only heard a little of it. He was always so proud of being a soldier. And in later years, he would go to the re-unions. Usually, he was what is called "THE LAST MAN STANDING". The oldest, year wise, that was there. Not age. I have never understood how he could be so mean to we 3 girls, but I think we were bad reminders of our mother. And nothing Santa Claus did that year was going to make it better.

A few months later, Dad had taken us to Virginia to live with his sister, our Aunt Sis.

Bless her heart; she had a lot of gumption to put up with us, especially me. I didn't trust anybody and I must admit I made their lives miserable. I resented the fact we were where we were. I didn't appreciate the fact I was in a loving home. My Aunt Sis was the greatest. Or maybe it was I expecting the rug to be yanked out from under me again. Her two daughters had to make the adjustment to us as well. And then Dad came after us with our NEW mother.

From the get go, she told us she wasn't our mother and not to call her "mother" which was fine with me but confusing. We rode the train to Virginia but rode the greyhound bus back to Texas. I guess it was cheaper. But it was so tiring. I got a great big blister on the back of my heel. Most painful and Dad did ask the driver to wait while we went to the doctor. The good doctor lanced the blister and gave Dad some medicine and off to the bus we went. Very much relieved. On the road again. I practiced saying her name "Rose" out loud. and I did call her by name, and there were a few times when I called her names I would have been fed a bar of soap for.

She didn't bother calling us anything unless it was some nasty name. And the awful names she called Dad. Well!!! Of course, it was always behind his back. I think she spent most of her time planning what to do against us. And it started from day one.

The time came, after the divorce that we all piled into the car. A 1941 Chevy, and off we went. Across the good old U.S. of A. I cannot tell you what the country looked like. Dot got the passenger seat in the front and Nancy got the whole back seat to stretch out on while I got the floorboard. Because I was little and fit in the half of the floor and used the hump as a pillow. It did get awfully tiresome not seeing anything. And I got so stiff. After awhile you would have thought Dad would have gotten tired of my belly aching but if he did, he never said a word to Nancy about sharing the seat. Then at night, we would stop in a roadside park, and the only thing that changed was Dad's spot. He slept on a picnic table. Dot got the whole front seat, and Nancy got the back seat. And you know where Gladys slept.

Just after Dad and Rose got married, Rose's daughter, Belen, was pregnant with her first child. Being curious, I asked her what the pills were that she was taking. She said they were vitamins and said I could take one. The minute I swallowed it, they all started laughing and saying over and over, "Gladys is going to have a baby". I started crying thinking that's how you got babies. When she had her baby, I wanted nothing to do with it. I never got over their cruelty. I can't say I remember them pulling practical jokes on Dot or Nancy.

When we got close to Virginia, Dad did spend some money for a rooming house, so we could all have a good night's sleep and a hot bath. He wanted us to look decent when we got to Norton and our grandparent's house. We stayed for about 2 weeks and then we were off again to Washington D.C. When we finally arrived, we had a major problem. No place to stay. Dad finally found a temporary place called Haines Point. A little motel. You weren't allowed to stay for a long length of time. But it worked while Dad was looking for a different place. I remember staying in a rooming house downtown.

Dad talked like a Dutch uncle to get them to rent us a room. Then he was off to the new job and looking everyday for a new home. The ladies running the rooming house were very nice and I guess felt sorry for three motherless little girls. They even gave me a Scarlet O'Hara doll they had kept from Gone With The Wind. I kept her until I got married and left it at Dad's house for safekeeping. When I asked for the doll, Dad said, "I don't know where it is. I haven't seen it for years." He did finally find a house in Landover Hills, Maryland. We settled in for what we thought would be a different life. We didn't have a stick of furniture in it, to speak of. A dining room table and chairs, 3 beds and a couch. My bed.

We grew up as young ladies, of course. We had manners and tried to be what he wanted us to be, I think. Girls he could be proud of. It was all for show. I can look back now and think, "Why did I try so hard to mimic him? Walk, talk, and even swear like him? I had a school friend come up and ask me why I always talked about my father and never my mother. I just plainly said, "I don't have a mother just a father." Never once did I use the word divorce. They seemed to accept it. I was ashamed of the fact they were divorced and she wasn't around.

When it came to school, I really enjoyed learning but wasn't a good student. I tried hard but for some reason it seemed to come hard to my brain. When I set my mind to a project, I always got a good grade. We had to do Silas Miner and I spent weeks doing a book report. I cut out magazine pictures to go with the characters in the book. It ended up being quite long. I got double A's and very good comments in the margins. I couldn't see very well because I needed glasses but didn't know it so I faked it. Probably why I had a hard time retaining.

The classes were always allowed to take field trips once a year. Usually the last part of the year. We went Annapolis, or to the zoo, or to downtown D.C... The trips to the government buildings were always fun. I remember our Biology class went to the medical museum. Not my idea of fun. To see all the medical abnormal babies or other medical problems in bottles just didn't set well with me. The teacher had made up a list of things we were supposed to look for and put the answers on the paper. I must admit I don't remember much of what I saw. Now the Botanical Gardens, that was different. I was a freshman that year, and I wore a sun back dress and was a hit I must say. No bra. I guess I could say I was the very first one to go braless. I managed to pass that year.

I went on to my sophomore year. One of the requirements was home economics. You know, cooking and sewing type of stuff. I would have just as soon not have done that. But I had to learn to make an apron. I'm getting closer to what my life is going to be for many years. At the end of that year, June 25th to be exact, I met my future husband, Dave. I did start my junior year fully intending to finish high school. We got married on the very first day of that school year. I went to school for half a day and Dave picked me up and we got married that afternoon. Dave did have a three day pass and we had made plans to go to Ocean City for a short honeymoon. Dad didn't see fit to sign my paper of permission until after the three days were passed. So our "honeymoon" was spent in Dad's house and Dave getting up and going to camp and me going to school the next day. Dot was the only one who went with us to the church. The big Baptist church in Mt. Rainier Md. It was Dave, me, Dot and the Minister. That's all. But after Dad punched my face off with his Mason's ring, I vowed to get even with him. I did, I thought. By quitting school. In the long run, I didn't hurt anyone but myself. But 50 years ago, schooling wasn't pushed as much as it is now, or needed as much as today. Maybe it was all those years of suffering and my newfound freedom was more than I could handle. I felt free. I had told Dave that no man was ever going to do that to me again. I had had enough punches for a lifetime. I wanted my marriage to be the only one I have in my lifetime. And I really worked at being a wife Dave could be proud of. But the strange part is, he never said he was proud of me, even after I gave him two beautiful daughters. I was to assume it I guess. I wanted a compliment once in awhile. A dog gets a pat on the head for doing a trick.

There were times when I was little that we were taken to my Grandparent Paden's house in El Paso and all the family were there. My cousin, Alice, was always there and my grandpa was always making over her. I guess they thought because her daddy was killed in some kind of accident on the base, they needed to make it up to her. She got it all. Love, attention and got away with murder. While we three didn't get much except the bottom of a slipper.

My grandparents were stationed in Nebraska for a while and my mother was born there. She must not have been wanted by my grandmother because she didn't treat her very nice. My mother was a rounder. Always did whatever she wanted to do. Never obeyed the rules, which always seemed so contrary to my grandpa's way of living. He was a career soldier. Very regimented. My mother was wild and did things her way. My grandpa was stationed out west when Custer was making his last stand. My mother was always having a run in with grandma. Always locking horns. As she grew, they were transferred to Fort Bliss and she had such fun with all the men on the base. She met and went out with Dad for some time. But the Padens wouldn't let him come to their house. Didn't think he was good enough. So they met at different locations. One of the meetings when they thought they were safe, my grandpa came up. Don't know if by horse or by car, but he told Dad "if you are going to spend time with my daughter, maybe you should come to the house". Of course, he still wasn't accepted by grandma. By this time, my mother was pregnant with my oldest sister. But I found out later on in years, it wasn't my Dad's baby. But he was willing to marry her and make a respectable woman out of her. My grandma was so vindictive, she didn't want any of Red's kids there. I see the chain going down the line. The pattern of abuse going from one generation to another.

Even after we were old enough to remember, I can't ever remember any Paden coming to our house in Logan Heights. My Mother had two sisters, and two brothers. It took many, many years to locate one brother in Denver. When I called on the phone, I asked if this was the Paden residence. My uncle said, "Yes it was". I then asked him if he had a sister named Jo. And he said yes. I said, "Well, this is Gladys, the youngest of her first litter." He said "OH my Gosh" and he started calling my grandma to the phone. She got on and said, "We all thought you were dead"...I said not hardly. She said every time she asked Jo about us she always said she didn't know where we were. The sad thing is, grandma couldn't even remember our names. I did manage a running relationship with them for a few years after that but nothing serious or what can be called loving. I guess it was curiosity more than anything. On both sides. She kept me informed on grandpa's illness. And when he finally died, she did tell me about it. Then, out of the blue, my uncle Frank called one day. Telling me he was in the town we lived in at the time. And wanted to know if it was ok to come to my house. Of course, I was thrilled. He and his wife stayed a few hours we talked each other's ears off. And after that we kept in touch. And I did feel a bonding with him I hadn't felt before. In the Paden family, everyone had a nickname. Cornball names but I remembered his as "T Body". My uncle John's was "Bozo". He couldn't figure out how I knew that. I told him I remembered uncle John playing drums in a room above the garage. They had a dog named "Rags" All he would say was "amazing" They lived on Pershing Dr. He was happy for me and Dave and my family and that we had a good life. He wanted to know all about Nancy and Dot. I had to tell him their lives were pretty messed up because of his sister and he agreed.

He wanted to know where Dad was and how he was doing. I flat told him Jo could have had what Myrtle had if she hadn't done what she did. We were being honest with each other. When he left, we had both promised to stay in touch and we did until he died. It wasn't until many years later, when my mother was dying, did I find my Uncle Frank in Arizona. The girls my mother had by the man she committed adultery with, called me to tell me she was so sick. I told them there wasn't anything I could do. They said she was in the hospital and about to leave this old world. I told them I would try to come and see her and talked Dave into going to Salt Lake City to see her. Well, imagine my surprise when we got there and she was at the house, walking around with her oxygen. We stayed awhile and then we went home. About a year later, they called again and said this was it this time. Could we pay for it. I said "NO.". But they could ask the family. The girls said they didn't think they would be welcome to call. I said I would call and that's all I would do. My Uncle John was surprised to hear from me, and said he would do what he could do. My mother did die and my daughter and I went to the funeral. The day of the funeral one of my half-sisters came up to me with a very tall man, and said "Dad, this is Gladys". He grabbed my hand and wouldn't let go. He kept saying he had to talk to me, over and over. I looked him in the eye, or rather, as best as my 5 ft. stature would let me, seeing as how he was over 6 ft tall., and said there wasn't anything he had to say to me then or ever. Nothing would wipe out the fact that he was the man who ruined our lives. He sort of shriveled right there in front of my eyes, turned and walked away. He made a point of staying out of my way during the rest of the funeral. My mother was a Methodist and was buried by the L.D.S. (Church of the Latter Day Saints).

She had told me, years ago, that she was born a Methodist and would die a Methodist. She didn't have the money to be buried with so she had a pauper's funeral. Very simple and plain. The Deacon of the church came over to me and asked what my instructions were. I had told him I was a daughter when we got there. I looked at him and said I didn't have any instructions. That he needed to talk to the other girls. He said O.K. and off he went. My daughter, Berta, said she didn't feel anything for her when she looked in the casket. I told her that was all right. I guess she thought she was supposed to because she was her grandmother. I told her it didn't work that way. That was the one and only time she had seen Jo. She was as much a stranger to me as she was to Berta. The Deacon came over again and said it was time for the final viewing and did we want to go up? I said no. He said she had a ring on her finger, "what did we want done with it?" I said it wasn't my decision. I guess they buried it with her. We went back to her house for just a few minutes and then Berta and I came home. I cried quite a lot when I got home. Not for my mother but for what I never had. Peggy never saw her because she lived in Hawaii at this time. And there was no reason for her to come all the way to the mainland for the funeral. I called Dot and Nancy to tell them that chapter of our lives was over. I haven't heard from the girls since the funeral. We all tried to be civil and they asked me all kinds of questions about my life with our mother. I tried to be honest. I told them how she didn't take care of us, and they said their mother wouldn't do that. I said, "Well, since I was there and she was my mother, that made her OUR mother", "and she did do it". They said that Jo didn't have the first girl for well over a year after she left us. Wrong. She was pregnant when Dad came home from over seas. His wife was in the hospital having their first child while he was cheating with my mother. He was a despicable person. He was even arrested for molesting his own daughters. What a cad. My mother wasn't any better at picking a mate than my Dad.

During the time we lived alone with my mother, and Daddy was still over seas, I was loose alone to wander around Logan Heights trying to find something to eat .and I found a treasure. It was called a pomegranate tree. Of course, it was in a fenced yard. The fence was made of stone and was about 4 foot high. That made it about 3 feet taller than me. But those ripe fruits hanging on that tree was so inviting to a hungry kid. So I took all my strength to climb that fence and got myself some of those pomegranates. I peel off the rind and bit into the fruit inside, it was so good. Of course, there are a zillion seeds in one fruit. I took about 3 more fruits and headed for my house. The owner of the tree came out to confront me. The property was called "Paul's Café". I tried to act like I didn't see him but he stopped me and asked me if I had stolen his pomegranates. I said no of course. Try to picture a little girl trying to look innocent with all this beautiful red juice stain down the front of the ragged dress and all over my hands and face, saying I hadn't taken the fruit. I guess he realized I was hungry and said "ok" and sent me on my way. It was still stealing. But I thought I had put something over on him. I don't remember what he looked like but I do remember he was a very nice man. I guess he was Paul.

And then my Dad came home and all Hell broke loose. Not his doing but my mother was a selfish woman and did anything to get what she wanted. She used everybody. Even at the expense of her children. I guess there are some children designated to be born into families by accident and there never is any love. From what I learned later, she even sacrificed her own sisters and brothers to her cause. Some people just can't love.

Daddy would cry at the drop of a hat, because of the betrayal and

I guess he tried to do a better job. We never went hungry after he got home, but all three of us were afraid we would. We learned bad eating habits because we were afraid there wouldn't be enough to eat. Deep in my heart, I miss Dot so bad and I keep saying she didn't have to die as young as she did. It was like she willed herself to die. She did everything wrong. She knew she was packing on the pounds. I know for a fact that Dot took two peanut butter sandwiches everyday of her high school years for lunch. It never varied. I was different. I never took lunch. I don't remember Nancy taking a lunch either. But Dot would do everything in excess. She would send me to the store for a six-pack of soda. The large ones. I think they were 16 oz. size. And she would drink 4 of them. And this was before diet colas. If we bought do-nuts, she ate 10 of them. Which was putting weight on her rapidly. And the more weight, the more unhappy she became. She had beautiful hair and she learned to make what is called broomstick skirts and looked so nice. She would starch them so stiff, they would literally stand up by themselves. But she was so miserable, it didn't seem to help her. Those are the skirts I had to rent from her so I had something to wear. She charged me .50 cents a day. And not only that, she made me wash and starch and iron them. And they had better pass muster. If it didn't stand up by it's self, she would make me do it over. I did it because I thought I might want to borrow them again. She was so possessive of her things, she wouldn't turn loose of anything. She had a bathing suit that fit me and was so cute. I was going to a beach party with some of my friends the last day of my 8th grade year. She would not let me borrow it no matter what I did to tempt her. I don't know why she wouldn't except maybe she was mad because she wasn't going. That bathing suit rotted and she still had it years later. I ended up wearing an old swimsuit but I had fun anyway. But I got one of the worse sunburns of my life. I looked like a lobster. And I couldn't even think of anybody touching me.

It never mattered to Nancy. She went the other way about that time. She only went to school and when she got home, she stayed inside the house. She wouldn't do anything.

When we girls were growing up, it seemed Dot and I were closer than Nancy and I, even though Dot and I were always fighting and trying to kill each other, we always seemed to be there for each other. After she threw me out of her house a zillion times, I would wait for a month or two, and she would call me to talk. I always swore I would not go back or call her, I always did. Her birthday was Nov. 8th and mine was Nov. 22nd so we were cut from the same cloth. We both had Scorpio temperament. Always ready to fight, even if it meant it was between us. We could never understand why we were not loved. And if nobody loved us, we wouldn't show love to anybody. I knew it was wrong to feel this way but who was going to teach me otherwise. I tried to make a difference to my Dad for the way my mother had treated him. To commit adultery was one thing but to commit adultery while your married partner was overseas fighting a war and trying to keep you safe is another. I don't think, in my heart of hearts, I ever forgave my mother. I didn't hate her but I didn't love her either. But I had this Southern idea that families stayed connected. Maybe that's why I never really let go. I felt my life wasn't whole. One-half, the Paden half, had a gap. I started doing a family tree and found out I had been named Joe, after a long line of Jo's. The difference is the "E" tacked onto mine. It was Josephine this and Josephine that. Very rarely do I use the Joe. My mother's first name was Josephine. From what I could find out, the name goes back several generations. But I didn't want it. And strange as it may seem, Dot got her middle name of "May" Why would anybody name their kids after themselves when they didn't want them. Some kind of cruel joke.

Dot went with me to be married and I was at her wedding in Ohio. For two sisters we were closer than I realized. Nobody else in the family even bothered with us.

I never thought about how Nancy or Dot was affected by our mother until we got to Maryland and Dot started acting strangely and Nancy drawing into her shell. She went to school everyday and came home. But she never did anything differently. No going out after she got there. I guess she did homework but can't remember seeing her do it. She isolated herself from us and even when she went anywhere with the rest of us, she wasn't enjoying herself. Special occasions were not special to her. I don't ever recall her asking for anything for Christmas or being excited when she unwrapped a gift. I was always happy just getting the wrappings. I miss Nancy very much. I know we didn't have the happy go lucky life of children growing up, care free and being children. We all 3 were made to grow up to fast. She chose to move back to the only place she remembered as a child, where she had happy memories with our grandparents.

When I compare the two early episodes that messed up our lives, one was our mother and the other was Rose. I have to say they are both just as equal as far as destructive to our minds. One was betrayal of our mother and then comes Rose with all her cruelty. With the combination of the two, it's no wonder we all had problems. I was the luckiest of all. It took me a while to learn that people can love you for yourself. Dot and Nancy never accepted that. Every once in awhile I catch myself falling back into the old trap and way of thinking. And I have to stop and think. It's not that way. We don't have to live in the past and the past doesn't have to rule your life. I'm not perfect and I do fall on occasion. I do love Dave and I do love my family. I even loved my Dad. Even though he didn't love me.

I can only remember Nancy going to a movie once with me and the movie was "Valentino" I thought it was such a good movie. Nancy told me later she enjoyed watching me more than the movie, especially when it showed Valentino coming down the stairs to do the Tango. I didn't know I had reacted, but she said I sat straight up in my seat and didn't take my eyes off the screen. Oh, he was good looking. He was played by Anthony Dexter. But he could have been Valentino's twin. To me, he looked so much like the real Valentino, I could understand why, when the real Rudolf Valentino was alive, all women fell all over him. I learned very early to do things and go places alone. The movie was made in 1951, so you can see we girls didn't do a lot together.

This was one of the times Rose came back to the house. I can see myself trying to make myself smaller just to stay out of her way. We were growing up and really didn't need a "mother" or a sitter. We could take care of ourselves or so we thought. I would find any excuse to stay out of the house. I stayed out so late sometimes, I caught heck from Dad. One time my friend's family had invited me to go to Chesapeake Bay for a weekend and go boating. I had finally got Dad to agree to let me go and went to my friend's house to tell them but stayed to long. Boy, did I catch it. And not only that, I got grounded from the trip, I did something I had never done in my life. I begged and begged and begged some more. But it didn't work. So I cried all weekend. Even after I knew they were gone, I cried. I figured Dad would come in and beat the tar out of me, but he never did. Never figured out why he didn't. But he got his point across. It all seemed so un-fair. All the adult world. He believed kids were to be seen and not heard. Do as I say and not as I do sort of thing. And Rose was always waiting in the wings. When he was gone, she did her evil...

She would try to pull the same stuff as in Texas, but we had made up our minds that she wasn't going to do that to us anymore. If she wanted a fight, we would go down fighting. I decided she wasn't going to do much more to me. And that the time she came home with her friend and started to take everything out of the house. I saw her one time after that. Dave and I had been married for a short time and we went into D.C. to do some shopping. We went to the May dept. store and happened to run into her. She worked there. We told her we were married and she said "Oh yeah?" That was all. We finished our shopping and left. She may have gone back to Texas or died in D.C. I don't know. And really don't want to know. I just hope someday, somewhere, she will have to answer for the mistreatment of 3 little girls. I really have to call it what it was, torture, of 3 little girls.

I catch myself thinking of all the ways I could make her suffer. But I know in my heart, I couldn't do to her what she did to me. It would be my luck; the old girl is still alive. Nobody would want her. Not even the devil... Not long after we moved to Maryland, I decided I wanted to take music lessons. Didn't really know what type of music, just wanted to start something. Dad decided it was going to be accordion lessons because our mother played the accordion well enough to be professional. His way of thinking was he would show her we could play as well as her. But with one big hitch, it cost money to give 3 girls music lessons at the same time. Every week he would take us into D.C. for lessons. I really liked to play. I was learning to read music and beat a rhythm with my foot. Every week I was given a new song to practice. One of my favorites was "Merry Widow Waltz". I practiced until my fingers fell off and I pumped the bellows until I couldn't. I would hide out in the bedroom and go to it. Dot did her practicing but wasn't into it and Nancy would sit there and just listen. And listen, and listen. Then came the day we would go to the studio. I would be asked to show what I'd done during the week. Everything went well until the teacher would show me where I made a mistake. Then Dot's turn would come and the same thing happen. Some time during her performance, she would make a mistake. And then it came Nancy's turn. Guess what? She played the same songs, with the very same mistakes where I had mine and where Dot's mistakes were. Nancy was learning to play by listening...By ear so to speak. It was funny. After we would get done at the studio, sometimes Dad would take us shopping. This one particular day we were standing on the street while he made up his mind what to do. I saw something on the sidewalk next to the wall. I just meandered over and picked it up, I walked back to Dad and said, "Look what I found". It was a twenty-dollar bill. Dad grabbed it and said "I'll keep this right here for you, see, I'll put it right here in the corner of my wallet and I'll know it's yours" Never did it see it again. But I guess he bought groceries with it or maybe even paid for a music lesson with it.

I was getting into playing and feeling real confident. We had a few recitals and all went well. Of course, Dad wasn't there. Then one day he said he wanted to ask us a question. We all stood there waiting for the bomb to go off. He asked us if we really wanted to continue the lessons. We all knew he couldn't afford it, so we all said "no". I was really disappointed. I think I was using it as another refuge. I was happy and no one bothered me. And once again, it was gone. I know now that everything Dad did was to make him look good, especially in front of my mother. But like I said before, I think it backfired on him. She didn't care one way or the other. Once in a while he really felt good and we would go for a ride and this one day, we were out sight seeing. We were all feeling good and somehow the subject of Norton came up. We were all chattering at once saying we wished we could go see our grandparents. It was one of those feel good days. So it seemed like in unison we all said, "Let's go". We didn't have any clothes for changing or anything. But he went along with the gag. I kept saying, "Are we really going to grandpas?" And he said "yes". It was clear across Virginia. I just couldn't figure out what was wrong with him, he was in such a good mood. When we got there, most of the relatives came to the house, and they thought it was so funny Clarence doing such a thing. Of course, he took all credit. We let him. Back in those hills, no body did anything on the spur of the moment. So they all knew he was a sure, fired, dyed in the wool, city slicker. There was one lesson I learned from those hill folks of mine. I would always make sure my children would eat at the same table as me, not wait for the adults to finish and if anything was left, the children got something. Many was the time we were made to wait and the adults would eat and eat and then sit at the table and gab forever. While we kids would wait and getting hungrier and hungrier.

I do believe it was about this time I got a real interest in John Wayne. He was definitely my movie star hero. I think back on it and I do think it was because he looked like my Dad in his facial features. And even though my Dad was so rough and at most times, mean to us, I still respected him. And my Dad was a career soldier and John Wayne played a soldier to the hilt. I guess I got them confused into one. Every movie I heard was coming with John Wayne in it, I was saving my money for a ticket. I can't say I was happy with all of them but most were good in my book. When I got depressed and felt picked on, I would look at John Wayne. I always said I wouldn't marry a man wearing a uniform, but I met Dave, and that all went out the window. He was a soldier too and while he was still in the army, he had to pull guard duty and all the things that are expected of soldiers. I would walk down to the guard shack and give him supper. I would sit in the guard shack and when a vehicle drove up I would hide under the ledge of the window until they were inside the gate. If we had been caught, he would have faced a court martial and

I would have been shot as a spy I guess. This was during the Korean police action. And Dave was my knight in shining armor. My soul mate. Dave was a good mechanic and the army tried to get him to re-enlist as a sergeant in the motor pool. But he said "no". We were ready to be on our own and start our family.

All three of us girls had to grow up to fast. We tried to have parties and picnics etc. I was with Dave and Dot was with Mac and Nancy was with a guy named Richard from New York. It always struck me odd that Dad never said a word against the guys we brought to the house. Maybe it was because they were in uniform. He always respected them for serving their country. I don't know his way of thinking. We fed them tons of food.

And it seemed that every weekend we were feeding more and more of them. Sometimes they would bring cocoa and sugar from the mess hall in camp for fudge and sometimes Dave would start out with a full stock of bananas but never got to the house with anything but the stock. We made full Mexican dinners for them. The word was out. And I'm sure Dad went into hock to pay for the fixings. Of course, me being the youngest, I didn't know much about the cooking, but I helped and acted like I was grown up. The guys all treated me like the rest. Except one time my date didn't show up. It wasn't Dave. But they invited me to go along anyway. A picnic in the park. Don't know where the park was, but I had a miserable time. Never did that again.

By this time, things were almost serious with me and Dave. Nothing had been talked about so I guess Dave assumed it. He was sent to Delaware and I stayed home. A carnival came to the Catholic

Church, which was a block from my house. Some of the remaining guys from camp came by and asked us to go. We said yes and off we went, except Nancy. I have always been afraid of heights and never did like the Ferris wheel. But this one guy I was with bought a whole roll of tickets and when we came around for the ride to stop, he just handed a new one to the operator and off we went again. When we got to the top, he would start rocking the seat... Oh my gosh, not my idea of fun. I screamed and screamed, until my throat was raw. When we got home, Nancy asked me if I had fun. My throat was so sore, I couldn't speak. The first thing she said was, "you better tell Dave you went out with this guy". The next night Dave came up after coming back from Delaware and lo and behold, he couldn't hear. And I couldn't speak. Not good. We just sat there and looked at each other and me trying to get my nerve up to tell him I had gone to the carnival. It got later and later. About 11:00 p.m., he said he had to get back to camp.

I said ok and I stood up and thought,"it's now or never" I tried to talk to him about going to the carnival and he couldn't hear me. We were not communicating very well at all. But I managed to get enough out for him to understand it. When the trucks got to the gate of the camp, all the girls that lived in the area came running up and had to tell Dave I had gone out with someone else. I didn't know so many people were watching us and our friendship. One of the girls said she hoped we would break up and then she would try to go with him. As I said, I didn't think we were serious about anything. I knew I liked him. And he acted like he liked me. So from time to time, we were together whenever we could be. He would stop at the house and ask me to go with him into D.C. when he went for parts for somebody's car or truck. And even though we didn't have any money, we enjoyed each other's company. About a week after I first met him, he got a 30-day furlough. He went home to Ohio to visit with his family. Boy did I miss him. I wandered around lost. I scribbled his name on everything. Dave this, Dave that, Mrs. Dave Gartrell. Every way I could, I wrote it. I guess I was in love. Not having experienced too much love in my lifetime, I wasn't sure. I knew I was happy to be with him and spend my time with him. But I had no guidelines to go by. I wanted to be his wife.

After he got discharged from the army, we moved to Ohio. We lived with his grandparents for a while. All the time looking for a house all of us could live in. The one we found needed some work. So we set about scrubbing and painting. Berta was only about 2 months old and she had a cold. We didn't want to take her with us into all the paint fumes so we asked Granny to watch her for us. She was agreeable. When we got home, all hell broke loose. They decided to take her to the doctor. They went right by the house where we were and didn't stop to tell us.

They accused me of being a bad mother and on and on. I asked them what right they had taking her to the doctor without our permission. His granddad was really pushy and threatened to beat me up. Dave told him don't even think of doing that because then Dave would have to beat him up, and he didn't want to do that. I told him fumes or no fumes, we would move into the house as it was. I began to gather up all the baby's things and dumped them into

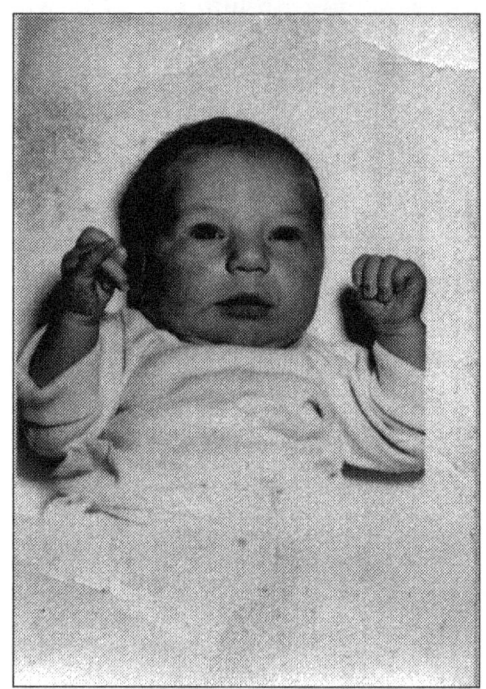

Peggy Ann

Roberta Jean

Gladys as a baby

Roberta & Peggy

Roberta & Peggy

W.C. Lovell, Dot and Gladys
Just before being shipped out.

Gladys with Doll, Dot and Nancy

Gladys with Doll

Dot, Nancy, Gladys and Mother, 1943

Dot and Gladys

Dot, Snooker, Gladys and Nancy

Dot, Gladys and Nancy

Nancy, Gladys and Dot

Dot, Gladys and Nancy

Peggy, Gladys and Berta, 1960

Peggy, Gladys, Berta and Dave, 1967

Grandma Lovell, Grandpa Lovell and Nancy, standing

Gladys and Dot

Nancy, Gladys and Dot

Nancy, Belen, Gladys and Dot

Gladys in High School

Nancy, Gladys, Dot & Rose

My Dog Silver

My Sister Dot

My Sister Nancy

Rose Orzoco

Grandpa Paden

Grandma Paden

Josephine Paden Lovell

W.C. Lovell

Myrtle & Daddy

a suitcase. When we were leaving the house, I told them to take a good long look, because it would be the last time they saw their great grand daughter. I meant it. I wouldn't have anything to do with them for a long time. Finally, Dad came by one day with some diapers for her and I invited him in. He was happy and all was over for that time. We managed to get along really well after that. Maybe it cleared the air. I know Berta loved them, as did Peggy when she came along. I would take both of the girls over to see them a lot. And there were times when the old folks got sick, sick enough sometimes to have to go the hospital. And I would take care of them. One time Dad was staying with us and he was suffering from Parkinson's disease and we lived on a farm that did not come up to standard when it came to plumbing and we had an outhouse. This day I heard Dad yelling for me so I went to look out the window to see what he wanted. Well, there he stood, with his pants down around his ankles. He had gone to the outhouse but couldn't get his pants back up because of the Parkinson's. I went out and pulled them up for him and as I pulled his suspenders up, I tried to make a joke out of it so he wouldn't be so embarrassed by what happened. He really was a sweet old man Granny was one tough old gal. But after I got to know her I think she liked me as I did her. She was the one who raised Dave when his Mom was working as a nurse.

His mother lived in Dayton and worked everyday as a nurse. She only had one child and her mother and dad did the raising of him. They always lived and worked on farms. They always had a morbid fear of another depression. They had lost everything during the hard times. Dave always acted like he loved his mother and insisted I go to the doctor she worked for when I thought we were going to have another baby. Over the years, I was always secure in my feelings with her. Most mothers with an only child feel there aren't any people good enough for their child. But she never made me feel that way. I asked her what she wanted me to call her, and she said whatever made me feel comfortable. So I said if it was all right with her, I would call her "Mom". She said that would be fine. And that was 48 years ago.

I don't know why, but I thought my life would be a fairy tale after I got married. I was a hands on mom. Always doing with, not just sending the girls off, to do for themselves. Like the room mother bit and scout leader and doing the camp outs. I even tried to work. I worked for two newspapers as a reporter and worked as a salesperson in a flower shop. I made sure the girls went to church, even though I didn't go with them. I could tell they were learning by just listening to them talk. And one day I over heard them talking in their bedroom about their Sunday school lesson that day. I stopped when I heard what the Minister's wife had told the kids about how God had made Eve for Adam by spitting in the dirt and stirring up mud and made Eve. I asked them if they were sure about what they had heard and both said yes. I said, "That's it". You're not going back to that church again. My neighbor went to the Minister and told him what I said. The next Sunday his wife stood up in front of the whole congregation and said she had tried an experiment with the kids to see if anyone was listening and I was the only one who caught it.

She was so proud of the girls and me as well. Can you beat that??

I was so proud of my girls. I was always proud of my girls; I nearly busted my seams whenever they were in anything. I really enjoyed learning about tribes of Indians in our country while they were earning their badges. We learned a lot but I bet the girls can't tell you much about them by now. And when special days came for scouts to be in the parades, I was there rooting them on the loudest. Dave was always there when he could be. I have always been the loudest cheering section for the girls and Dave. I tried to get them ready for growing up girl things and thought that was the way it should be. But our Peggy, who I thought had understood it like Berta, came home from the first day of school, went into the bathroom and locked herself in. After about an hour, Berta came and sat down on the arm of my chair, and very grown up said "Mom, Peggy started her period today". I thought "oh no". I went and knocked on the door. She said, "Leave me alone". I said, "Come on Peggy, open the door. You're among friends here you know". I went in and gave her a hug and began to help her. In a little while, it was over and she went back to being my tomboy. She did ask me as few days later how long this went on. I said only a few days but actually the rest of your adult life. She said "oh my gosh, I'm so tired of wearing this Mickey Mouse mattress". I nearly cracked up. She was never afraid to explore. A lot like me, I guess. And she didn't let growing up stop her.

When the girls were little, I would make costumes for them for Halloween. I fell back on what I had made when I was a kid. Once I went as a bubble dancer. I spent money on balloons that afternoon and the rest of the day blowing them up. And sewing them onto a bathing suit. Got it all done and dressed and it was so cold, Dad did decide to drive me to the carnival. It was held outside and it started to drizzle rain. All the boys kept trying to see under the balloons. The judging took a long time and I got so cold, Dad stayed and covered me with his jacket. He probably thought I was going to get pneumonia. Well, it was worth it. I won first place! As soon as it was over, Dad started breaking balloons with his badge and hustled me into the car to go home. I got in a hot bath and soaked for the longest time. Another time I made a costume of an Indian. I used a fringed bed spread as the main part of the costume. I had beaded bedroom slippers made like moccasins, and for braids, I used nylon stockings. I braided them into two separate braids. Looked real enough. Then came the best part. The make up. I used Ox blood colored shoe polish. Did all of my face and the tops of my feet and hands. Looked good. Again, I won first place for originality. But the polish didn't come off so easy. And then about three days later, I broke out in a mess of a rash. I still had the red color about a week later. But it was worth it. I'd won. Another one was a scarecrow. Using Dad's coveralls and an old army fatigue hat, we stuffed straw into the coveralls, and out the hands and feet. Won again. So mainly these ideas worked when my girls were dressing for Halloween. With some new ideas. One was a clock and since I smoked Tareyton cigarettes, I used the pack as an idea. I stood some cigarettes in stages of coming out of the pack and Peggy was the tallest cigarette. She wore a half mask. Most people would ask, "Well, does she?" "Would she rather fight than switch?"

She would lift her mask and Bingo, she had a black eye. They would laugh. They usually won a prize. It was a job but fun. They always seemed to have fun doing it. I was always there with them, rooting them on. I wanted them to have good childhood memories. I wanted them to remember being a family.

The time came for what Dave thought was the girls being grown up enough to give up the idea of old Santa. I had always done all the gift buying during those years and was busy wrapping everyone's presents to put under the tree. And out of the blue, he called them into the living room. He said "Berta and Peggy, I want you to meet Mr. And Mrs. Santa Clause" and pointed to him and me. They just sat there and looked un-believing. Peggy started crying and said "no". I felt sorry for her. I guess she still believed in her little heart. It took some of the magic out of it. I know it took all my sneaking and hiding out of it. No more letters to Santa. One more step toward adulthood.

When there were field trips from school, I would volunteer to go with the class and make all kinds of goodies for all. We would go to the Cincinnati zoo, or other interesting places. And the kids learned something. While a scout leader, I planned a night at the Cincinnati Gardens to see Holiday on Ice. Very interesting and pretty to watch. The first year we only had one bus, the next year two buses, and by the third year, we needed three buses. But a good time was had by all. I assigned bus monitors and made sure all were accounted for. Each girl was to bring their own refreshments from home. That way nobody was running loose and we all made restroom runs as a group. Sure didn't want to misplace any of my girls. All worked out great and we all got home together, tired and sleepy but happy.

As the girls grew, they went through the usual childhood diseases, Chicken pox, measles, rubella and mumps. And so did Dave. After awhile he said, "I wish theses kids would keep their germs to themselves". For the most part, they were easy on the girls. But for Dave, it was very hard. Especially the mumps. That all happened while we lived in Lanham. First Berta got the mumps along with 2 ruptured eardrums. And then Peggy got them. While trying to take care of two sick kids, I came down with the Hong Kong flu. One night while Dave was trying to fix all of us supper, he said he felt a funny feeling behind his ears. I told him not to worry, he had the mumps. He said, "No I don't" The next morning I felt him sneak out of the bed to go to the bathroom. He tried creeping back into bed without waking me. I said, "Do you have the mumps?" He turned his face around to me and said, "What do you think?" His face was swelled up, huge, on both sides. I started laughing so hard the tears ran down my face. Poor guy wasn't feeling well at all. So to make sure he didn't move fast or do much, I got out of the sick bed to take care of him. Which was a good two weeks. It was his turn to be taken care of. He hurt a lot. That year, everyone around the area came down with the flu or something else nasty. There wasn't a soul we knew who wasn't sick. It was epidemic. We decided to go back to Ohio. Dad said "don't you know a rolling stone gathers no moss?" I ask, "Who needs moss?" That's when our true migration west started. We never moved back to Maryland. We steadily moved west.

First we stopped in Ohio and settled there and became friends with some of Dave's old school mates, Don and Alice, Dick and Betty, Paul and Ginny and Danny and Frances. We would all get together in the evenings and play all kinds of games. One in particular, called "Aggravation" would get pretty heated. And I really felt sorry for

Alice because if Don was losing, Wham! He would kick her under the table. We all learned pretty fast why it was called Aggravation. Then we would play " Shanghai rummy." Now that game got real hostile. It called for some extra hard hands. Tempers flew. There were times when we wives wouldn't speak to our men for days. All the while, we were doing our thing, the kids, and there were boo-coo kids, were playing and having lots of fun. I don't remember them ever having any serious problems. They all grew up together. We would pile into our cars and go to Greenville to the fair. The kids went one way and we went another. We knew we could find the men at the farming equipment or animal barns. After about 4 or 5 hours, we would gather up the younguns and head for home. The kids would be so dirty you could only see the whites of their eyes. And I could place a safe bet they would be asleep before we got 5 miles down the road.

The next year was time to think school. And we got Berta ready to go. The first day of school, I took her to her class. I asked her if she would be all right riding the bus home and she said yes, feeling grown up. So I went home. That afternoon I waited. I saw the bus go by and no Berta, I waited some more. The bus went by again and still no Berta. So I thought, "I will wait for one more bus and if she isn't on it, I'll go to school". Well here comes one more bus and I see Berta sitting on the bus not making any effort to stop the driver. I flagged him down to see why she hadn't gotten off. She said she liked riding the bus.

I thought it was 3 different buses but it was the same one. She had gone round 3 times. The driver said he kept asking her where she lived and she wouldn't say anything. He thought it was funny .He remembered where she lived from that time on.

Dot and Mac were trying to be happy and Nancy came to Ohio to live with us. Since Dot and Mac didn't have a baby yet, she stayed with them. Nancy and I went to work in a plastics factory. They made little toy trucks to go in Post cereal boxes. The trucks came in models of flatbeds, tankers, low boys, and box trailers. There were hundreds in a box and it wasn't so bad as long as it was the tankers and box trailers. But when it came to the flatbeds and low boys, there were twice as many in a box. The cars were Ford models. And then they decided to put boats in. We had to snap them together. Talk about sore fingers. And because it was a food product, we had to wear hairnets. There was only one man on the shift and we women didn't feel any pity for him. Nancy had worked there longer than me so one night I asked her why Carl was always going into the men's room. She said that's where he keeps his booze. He would keep it in a coke bottle and would go in and take a swig. I guess he needed fortification with all of us. He was called a foreman but he lost control a long time ago. We girls all laughed and told jokes while we put on wheels. We had a system of laying the trucks in the palms of our hands and pick up a hand full of wheels and roll them onto the trucks. The wheels would snap into the brackets. And we would pitch the finished trucks into the boxes and grab another bunch. We always did our quota by the end of our shift. but Carl didn't think so. So he started separating us. I eventually ended up in the grinding room where the excess plastic that was cut off the toys was re-ground and melted down to be remolded into more toys.

The grinder top was higher than my head and would jam with sharp pieces. I asked Carl, the boss, how do I un-jam it? He just said use you hands and move it around until it loosens it. I said "OH no, these hands came is as a set and they are going out as a set." "Where is the main power switch and I need a stick as a jabber." He just said I was being foolish but he showed me main switch and the next day I had a big stick standing by the machine. By the end of the shift, I was covered with plastic dust.

During all this, Dave was teaching me to drive. We were driving down the road when I came to a corner. I said, "What do I do?" He said, "Turn". I did, but I didn't let go of the steering wheel. And around we went. You know, let the wheel slide back easy like, through your hands until it comes back to the original place. He caught up with it just inches from a power pole. Another time he was on my case about doing it like he wanted me to. WRONG!!! We were downtown Washington, D.C. at that time. Cars and trucks and even trolley cars all around us. He made me so nervous, I just got out of the car, and got in the passenger side. Dave said, "What are you doing?" I said, "Not driving, you do it". He learned to be a little more patient with me after that. When we got to Ohio, Dot and I, thinking we were true drivers, set out from Dave's grandparent's house in a little Ford coupe. Knowing Dad didn't want anyone to drive over his grass, I said, "I can do it" so I started backing out of the barn, I zigged and zagged. I couldn't get the darn car to go where I wanted it to go. I kept doing this all the way to the edge of the lane. I kept zigging and zagging across the lane. Never touching grass or fence. This went on for quite some time. Then Dot and I saw Dave and Mac coming down the road heading for the lane. We both jumped out of the car and ran in different directions.

I don't know where she went but I headed for the hayloft in the barn. I stayed in that loft for hours and wouldn't come down. Finally, Dave came and talked me down. He had only one question, "how did you get that car in the lane like that?" It took him awhile to get it out We never did see Granny or Dad during all of this but I bet they were in the house laughing their heads off. And wondering what kind of girl their grandson had married. I decided I need a few more driving lessons. Mainly backing up.

I finally quit F & F Mold and Die works because I was on second shift and didn't get off until midnight. Which meant I had to get Berta from Dot's. I had to get her out of bed and out into the cold and go home. This was in January and early February of 1956. I became pregnant immediately. And about that time, Dot found she was pregnant too. The two of us spent the time having a good time getting ready for our babies. Her's was due in November and mine in December. Dot had an easy pregnancy and was very happy. Mine wasn't. From the get-go, I was in a bad way. Sometimes so sick I couldn't get out of bed. But I didn't worry because I had already had a baby. We shopped for baby things when we had a few dollars. Then we would take them home and sit for hours just looking at them. Anxious for the babies. Then Dot's time came. And almost from the start, things didn't go right. She was in labor for hours. The baby came down into the birth canal but wouldn't or couldn't go any farther. After about 30 hours, the doctor decided to do a C-section.

The baby was pushed back up and the operation took place. The baby's head was affected. Her name was Vickie Lynn and she only lived a day and a half. I was still about 6 weeks away from having my baby. Dot was still in the hospital when they buried her little girl. Dave didn't want me to go to the funeral but I insisted on going.

All the while I was sitting there listening to the minister talking about how it was God's work and we weren't to question his wisdom, I was so thankful my baby was safe inside me. After the service, we went back to our house in Eldorado and Dave went off to do something outside. I decided to lie down for a while when all of a sudden, I hear a car go by. I looked out the window and saw a car going by that had been harassing me for months. I called Dave in and he went out the door flying. Never knew what this guy wanted but it got so bad, I wrote down his license tag number and the description of his car. I wouldn't let Berta play outside unless I was with her. But after just coming home from that funeral and feeling on the verge of a total wipe out, seeing him that day was more than I could take. Dave chased him over Preble County but couldn't catch him. We figured he was up to no good or he wouldn't have run, but we never saw him again after that .When I first noticed him, I was about 3 months pregnant, and Berta and I were out walking. Up the road from us was a roadside park. It had swings and slides and monkey bars. It was a good place to go for my exercise and Berta could play on the equipment. Then after hanging around for a couple of hours, we would walk back home. One day I thought it strange I kept seeing this same Pontiac. So the next day I paid special attention to it. I mentioned it to Dave that night at supper. He said it was probably someone who lived around there on one of the farms. I said, "You are probably right" and really didn't think anymore about it. I would see the car every occasionally, but didn't take it seriously. One day there was a knock at the door. I answered it and there he stood. It surprised me so much, I couldn't think. He asked me if I had any sweet potatoes for sale. I could feel myself getting very scared for me and for Berta. I told him "NO" and closed the door.

I have always had the habit of locking my doors, so the screen was hooked. I had so much trouble with my pregnancy and now emotionally, this guy upset set me so bad, I started having trouble with my eyes that night. I tried to read and before I knew it, the less I could see. It started with big black spots in my eyes. Dave was working night shift and the longer it went, the less I could see. In this little old house, we still used a hand crank phone. I managed to get to the room with the phone by feel, crank the phone handle and wait for Nancy to come on. She was working there at the time as an operator. I told her I was having trouble seeing and for her to call Dave. When he got on the phone, I broke down and told him I couldn't see. He came right home and we headed for Dayton and his Mom's apartment. When she opened the door, she asked me "what in the world happened?" I really couldn't tell her because I didn't know myself. She settled me on the sofa and called Dr. Rust. He told her to take me to the office and run a lot of tests. On our way across Dayton to the office, Dave jumped a traffic light and got pulled over. The cop asked him "where do you think you're going? To a fire?" Dave said, "No, my wife is sick and we are going to the doctor's office". The cop shined his light in the car window at me and saw my stomach and said, "Go ahead Dave but be more careful." "And good luck". And off we went. The doctor was calling on the phone by the time we got to the office. Mom told him about our wild ride and did the tests. The doctor thought I was having Toxemia or something else serious. He told her I was to come back in the next day for a more complete checkup. I did and the first thing he said to me was "what's this I hear about you going on big toot and getting blind sided?" He asked me all kinds of questions and said everything was looking ok. So he sent me home to wait. I was miserable. I would be so hungry but when it came time to sit down to eat, I couldn't.

Peggy was finally born, she weighed 71/2 pounds and I had only gained 9 pounds the whole 9 months. She was healthy and a bouncer. I was much luckier than Dot. But the doctor said No more babies. When I had Berta, I was one week away from my 18th birthday and had just turned 20 when Peggy was born. So I had a lot on my plate. A wife and a mother of two. It all started to weigh me down. I would take care of my kids all day but the minute Dave came in the door, I turned the kids over to him. I wouldn't do anything. I would go lock myself in the bedroom. And I mostly wouldn't go shopping. I cried at the drop of a hat. Dave didn't know what to do for me so he took me to the doctor and he called it postpartum depression. And if I didn't get a grip on it, it would only get worse. That nobody can help Gladys but Gladys. To make myself get out. Go to the store with Dave even if I didn't want to go and didn't get out of the car. Stay in the car and let him take the kids in the store and get the things we needed. I really think the two of them conspired to get me out of the car by acting dumb and forgetting half of what I sent him in for. He knew me well enough to know eventually I would go into the store and get the things we needed for the girls. Dr. Rust said it was a lot for a young person to do. At first, it was only me and Dave and the dog. Then all of a sudden I had two children, a husband, a house and a dog. A lot of responsibility. After awhile it got easier. I've always tried to remember what the doctor said about helping myself. There have been several times when I could have used a shoulder to cry on. A big hug. Someone to tell me it was going to be all right.

About this time, after I was feeling better, the girls were outside playing. I heard a small voice yelling "Mommy" so I went to the window to see what she wanted. Why I went to this one window to look out, I'll never know. But it looked out into the backyard and the outhouse.

I could see into the outhouse because the door was open. There was Berta holding onto Peggy under the arms, around the chest and yelling for me. Peggy was about 2 inches away from being dropped into all that mess in that pit. I yell, "don't drop her" and took off running for the door. I got there just in time because I don't see how Berta could have held her much longer. I grabbed Peggy and got her up and out of there. After a hug and a cry, I asked Berta what she was trying to do? She said there was a little rabbit down there and she threw the toilet paper in trying to chase it out. And then she wanted to save the toilet paper. Oh Lord, Peggy would have suffocated. I told Berta not ever do that again. We can always buy new toilet paper, but we couldn't get another Peggy...

Back during the time Dave and I were going together, we were sitting on the front porch and talking about our plans. Not our plans together, just plans in general. I was talking about how I would never marry a man who was married before. He asked "why?" I said, "If a man can't get along with his then wife, he certainly couldn't get along with me. I went on rattling about my plans to have two baby girls and out of the blue Dave asked if I'd picked out names yet. I said I hadn't gotten that far. He said "what about the name Leita?" I said I didn't like it. We went on to a different subject. The day came for us to go to Upper Marlboro, Md. for marriage license. After waiting in line with lots of others, mostly service men and their brides to be, and getting all kinds of well-intentioned advice about me being so young, we finally got to the front of the line. Then the clerk asked the usual questions, name, address and have you ever been married before? I said "no" and Dave said "no' as well. It wasn't until many years later, that questions came back to haunt me.

One night after we had gone to bed and were doing our usual chitchat before going to sleep, I asked Dave if he wouldn't like to have a son. He said, "I already have one out there somewhere". I said, "What are you talking about?" All of a sudden, it was soul-cleansing time. He decided to tell all. He decided to confess he had been married before and had a son. I was flabbergasted. I was glad it was dark in our bedroom so he couldn't see my face. I was so hurt at the betrayal of his lying to me. Things came back into my memory... When we were waiting for our first daughter to be born, I had wanted her name to be Jaymie Jean, but Dave had said he wanted Roberta Jean. He won, as usual. I tried to stay calm that night and told him maybe when the baby grows up he will try to get in touch with Dave.

We had a full conversation over this. I finally we to sleep and tried not think about it. Maybe I should have pushed for more answers. Later years proved I should have.

Many years later, we were sitting in the living room when our phone rang. I answered it and a man's voice asked if this was the Gartrell residence? I said yes it was. He asked if Dave Gartrell lived there and I said yes, and I asked who was calling? He said Terry Winter. I started to hand Dave the phone, thinking it was somebody from the mine. Then all of a sudden, I felt sick to my stomach. I started sweating and shaking all at the same time. I didn't know why but something told me we didn't want this phone call. My female instinct said, "Run." I couldn't hear but one side of the conversation but I could tell he was telling Dave things about being related or something. I finally told Dave to stop talking and tell me who and what this was all about. He said it was some guy claiming to be his son. He talked some more and after awhile, he offered me the phone saying he wanted to talk to me. I took the phone and proceeded to tell him, whoever he was, and if he was Dave's son, he went about it all wrong. How did we know if what he said was true? He should have gone through a third party and found out if Dave even wanted him in his life. Not come blasting into our lives and tearing us all up. There were more people involved than just him. After a week of this garbage going on between me and Dave and not getting anywhere. I told him he had to tell Berta and Peggy and it was him doing the telling. And it better be the truth and no more lies. Terry said he would send proof over to us. and he did. His real birth certificate and a whole bunch more. That's when it clicked in for me again. While reading those papers, I see two names that floored me again. Leita and Robert Paul. No wonder Dave wanted her named Roberta. But he kept denying that he ever told me he had a son.

Years ago, he did. It was another lie. Selective memory. I have always believed you don't break faith with your partner, no matter how hard it is sometimes, you have to be honest. When you first meet and start going with someone, you start with faith. Then comes love. and after awhile they just blend together. I think Robert and Roberta, not a coincidence. I have spent hours thinking about this. I can't believe how Dave can think this is his right to do this to me. Yet he will condemn others without a second thought. It seems to come easy to him. I struggled with the news about Terry for months, and finally came to the conclusion I couldn't keep Dave and his son apart. I didn't ask any more questions. I was afraid of the answers I guess. I had started to doubt. I figured I had lived with these lie, not mine, his, for almost 40 years. I guess I could do it longer. So after I finished my crying and the pain died down some, I got busy on the phone and tried to act civil and set up a date with Terry, Dave and Berta in Utah so they could meet each other. I didn't want to, but I would do the best I could. We went to their house in Dinosaur, Utah .And when we got there, Terry had another one of his siblings he had recently located at his house, as well as his family. I took every one out for a nice dinner and I paid for everything. You know what? Not one person said thanks. The bill was well over one hundred dollars. I decided then and there, if they wanted to know each other better, it was going to be up to them. I went into the restroom and looked at my face to see if the word "STUPID" was written on my forehead.

Of course it wasn't. I think it happened because I couldn't think of another person going through life, not knowing who he was. Terry's mother had been married 5 times and after going through life as an only child, he suddenly found out he had 10 brothers and sisters. The new siblings he found began to over whelm him and abusing his hospitality.

Peggy never met him and would just as soon not. It isn't pushed. I think there are some babies born who go through their whole lives and never know any true love from people we pick. I think after all these years it got to be a habit. I got the impression in later years Dave didn't feel for his own mother like I thought he did. Maybe he resented her for not raising him. Maybe he felt she dumped him on her parents. Back in those days, 30 miles from Dayton was a safe distance to make sure nobody found your secret. People weren't as mobile then. But I can't begin to tell you how much I have always loved Dave. And how much it hurts me when I find out all the little secrets. I hate secrets. They hurt everyone. They betray not only the people who do the betraying, but also the innocent ones. I guess Dave thought it would always stay hidden. Oh, what a tangled web we weave when we practice to deceive.

I blame myself for most of this. I guess I was afraid I couldn't do anything on my own because I was married so long. I had no confidence even though I had worked some outside jobs. I just let Dave do whatever he wanted to do. I felt if we stayed married and gave the girls a good home, that's all I could expect. But I did expect more. I wanted love. I wanted a kiss on the cheek every once in awhile, and a big hug and a little compliment thrown in for good measure.

If I tried to hug, it always ended up in sex. And that was supposed to make it all better. A little comfort for my pain would have been nice. Even the kids got comfort for their owies. I have always tried to be strong and supportive for Dave and my kids but some times it was hard. I'm not saying it was all bad, it wasn't. We had more good times than bad when they were growing up. But it seemed like it was always things the girls had planned or Dave. If I said I wanted to do something, like go to a show or just go somewhere, it was always asked "why?" I didn't go to a show for years.

One time Dave was planning on going on a hunting trip with his buddies out to Colorado. My friend Melita was at our house having a cup of coffee. Dave was busy giving me orders about what to do or not to do. And an important order was I was to be in the house after dark. Melita said, "Can she go if I go with her?" He said, "Yes that's ok". I was never so embarrassed in my life. He thought I needed a babysitter. He thought I was smart enough to be left with two small children, but not smart enough to go out by myself at night. Oh well, forget about it and go on. The trouble is, you don't forget. Like I said, I love him dearly, but there have been times.

During the time we lived in Tennessee, Dave worked for a timer's factor, named Smithville Controls. It usually was a Monday through Friday workweek. It was a new factory getting started and Dave helped to set it up. It had been brought down from Kokomo, Indiana. They made timers for washers and dryers. Being new, when a truckload was boxed up, Dave and I would drive them to Marine City, a suburb of Dayton and every time we checked in the gate, the guard said, "The lady has to stay in the truck". After off-loading the timers, we would go to Mom's house and spend the night. We made many trips to Dayton. Then the company asked Dave to work over time on a Saturday. I went over to Dad's but was uncomfortable while I was there. The sixth sense was working over time on me. I told Dad I had to go home. He asked why because I had just got there. I said I didn't know why I just had to go. When I got there, I set my ironing board up in the living room, right next to the phone. The phone rang and I grabbed it before it finished the first ring. A voice said, "Gladys, this is Jim. Don't panic, but Dave's been hurt. I said, "Ok I won't". Jim said, "Don't panic but I'm at the hospital with Dave" I said "I wont" And for the third time Jim told me not to panic. I asked, "Who is this?"

He said "Jim Puckett'. I guess I had mentally braced myself after the first "don't panic". He told me Dave's hand had been hurt bad but not how bad. And he was at the hospital with Dave. Dave told Jim to tell me not to come to the hospital... I thanked Jim and got the girls into the car and drove to Dad's. Left the girls and drove to the hospital. When I got to the room, Dave asked how I got there so fast. I thought I was moving in slow motion. Dave said a machine had pulled his thumb off. He wouldn't let me see it and he was very depressed. As it happened, we had planned a vacation for the next weekend. The doctor wouldn't let him go right then, and when the last of the stitches were removed, he told us to go on our trip and what to do to take care of it. Still Dave wouldn't let me see it. The weather turned off very bad. Rained everyday, ice, and just plain miserable. I was cooking on park picnic tables. I would get drenched with the rain, but figured it would help Dave to be doing what we had planned. The rock-hunting trip. One night, while he was changing the dressing on his hand, he asked if I was ready to see the ugly thing? His words not mine. I thought "oh dear" but if he was ready for me to see it, I'd better be ready to, so I had to be brave and go look. I mustered all my courage and went into the camper. I can't begin to tell you how happy and relieved I was when I saw Dave's hand with a half of a thumb. I had pictured the whole thumb being gone. I thought it had been torn off at the palm. It healed well. But because of my getting so wet and cold and maybe run down from the stress, I went home with pneumonia. I remember climbing into my bunk to shiver and shake all night. Never did warm up. Started running a high fever and didn't feel well at all. By the time we got home to Smithville, Dave was up and doing very well. It was me who went to the doctor and was put to bed.

This was really the worse injury Dave did to his hands. He cut the ligaments in his hand, he burned his hand so bad it damaged the nails, and when Berta saw him getting out of the car, she slammed the door shut and very dramatically pressed her body against the wall with her arms out on each side and said "oh no, he's done it again". I doctored him so often because of work related injuries, I started telling people I was so well trained, I was going to hang out my nursing shingle outside the door.

Even though I was born and partially raised in the south, I can't ever remember my Dad ever speaking ill of anyone. He had many bad faults but that wasn't one of them. He was from Virginia and not the most educated man in the world, book wise. His learning came from living. And I never heard him use the "N" word. So we never saw the difference in people. Living in El Paso, we were living side by side with the Mexicans but then we moved to D.C. and we lived close to the Blacks. I would get on the bus and head straight to the back seat of the bus. I never thought that's where black people were to sit. I just liked the big wide seat in the back of the bus.

Lucky Cantrell was, in my opinion, one of the most bigoted people I have ever met. He was always badmouthing people of different races, especially blacks. He kept this up for years. Knowing I hated it. He went home for a vacation and when he came back from Smithville, he handed me a card to read. It had on it "J. Lucky Cantrell is a full member of the KKK, and entitled to all rights and privileges." I just handed it back to him and didn't say a word. He said, "Well that went over like a lead balloon". I said, "If you want to be a jerk, be one. It makes no difference to me". But I knew he couldn't be KKK. They wouldn't let him in. He was part Indian

Only whites are allowed. Knowing how I feel about the Klan, he thought he would get as rise out of me. I told him a hundred years ago, he wouldn't have been allowed to marry my daughter. He asked "why?" and I said, "Because back then Indians weren't allowed to marry white girls. He said "oh". And after that, he pretty much kept that part of himself away from me.

I don't have anything against him. He is our granddaughter's father. I mean, we did get her from him. What went on between Berta and Lucky was their business, not for us to snoop in. As long as no one was getting beat up, we tried to mind our own business. That alone was a big job.

It wasn't long before Berta told us she was pregnant. She was carrying twins. But things didn't work out to be and she lost them. Lucky was working with Dave at the Victoria mine and Berta was working at the Gold Rush casino in Wendover, Nevada. Amanda had to ride the school bus about 47 miles to McGill for school. All the kids who lived in the valley did. So the days for the kids weren't easy. About this time, Dave was thinking about looking for a different job at a different mine. It was located west of Ely. It was about 120 miles or so out from town. For a while, Dave drove back and forth to town to get the mine bus. I would stay awake so I could talk him in on my C.B. radio. Helping him stay awake. I didn't want him to fall asleep driving home. He did that for about a year. And then we started looking for a house in either Ely or McGill. We couldn't find one in our price range so we looked for quite some time before we finally found one. In McGill. We lived there for 6 ½ years. Then we found a nice house with some land between the two towns. It was a big roomy house that we thought would work when the kids came to visit. And I would have a room for all my dolls. It has 13 rooms. Half of which we don't use. I always say we have the biggest doghouse in White Pine County because it's only me, Dave and our dog Jasmine. But we try to keep it up and Dave loves to dink and putter outside. We have a dune buggy and every once in a blue moon we go up into the hills to watch the deer and elk. We also have some not so welcome visitors. Rattle snakes. Not good. But desert is as desert does.

I guess when you're pretty much happy the years seem to go by fast. I still remember the girls doing all the things growing up and now the years have passed and its 50 plus years. Seems only yesterday I met and wanted to marry Dave. I don't think I was ever too un-happy.

I must have settled into a way of life I thought was good and acceptable for us. I can still see Peggy riding her itty-bitty 2-wheeler bike all over the place and she wasn't much bigger. She flew like the wind. Berta always being the stick in the mud.

Over the years, I would hear parents telling their kids how proud they were of them. , I heard compliments for Dave, Berta and Peggy but not a single compliment for me. I have tried many things, like knitting, doll making, painting with oils and this one project I thought I was doing pretty good. Because I sold a couple. No big prices just enough to make me feel good. Until Berta gave me her "critics" opinion. She didn't like them. I had learned to paint saw blades and personally, I thought I was doing good at it. I quit right then and there. And never painted again. I figured, what's the use. I did well with doll making and even gave one to Amanda as a keepsake. She didn't want it. I gave everyone in the family something I had knitted. I even knitted Dad a dark sweater to wear with his uniform. Not good enough. He did find the energy to tell me all that was wrong with it. I have yet to hear a "thank you"

I have trained dogs all my life. It was a self-taught thing I learned as a little girl. I was always the one who took care of them. And I always took them for their vaccinations to make sure they stayed healthy. I would teach them to sit and to stay and to heel. The usual stuff. I guess the pattern was set way back when I was young. Everyone would say, do it for yourself, but it was nice if someone did

notice. But I'm not a very good one to talk because I would tell Dot
the same thing. Do it for yourself. But she didn't listen to me either.

She was such a good interior decorator. She could take a shack
and make it into something so nice and eye appealing, and so nice.
She could sew very well. The only thing she couldn't do was handwork.
So every time I would embroidery a kitchen towel or do a doily, she
would latch onto it and put it in her "hope chest". Of course, by the
time I got married, I didn't have a single one.

But that's all right, I miss Dot so much. I sit and think of all the
struggles we three went through. And the last time she was in the
hospital. I had called Holly, her daughter. She had put Dot on the
phone and I was trying to talk to her. For some reason, she couldn't
hear me. She started crying so I told Holly I would talk to her later.
Little did I know that was going to be the last time I'd be able to
talk to her. She died the next day. Berta and I went back to Ohio
for the funeral. And since I have this terrible phobia about flying,
Berta got busy and got it all set up to go by Amtrak train. It wasn't
the best trip because I was thinking of Dot. And Berta didn't like
the train. It was her first train trip. She kept telling me if I'd just
fly, we wouldn't have to go this way. I've always thought when you
do something for someone, especially out of kindness, don't screw
it up with criticism. Say "no" to start with. I already felt bad that
wasn't helping. Then when we got to Ohio, it was in the middle of
the night. David, Holly's husband, and Jeff were there to pick us up
and take us to Castine. Mac had stayed home with the kids. It was
about 30 miles from Hamilton to Castine and we were talking and
I asked how Dad was doing? Both David and Jeff were quiet and

finally David said "their gone". Both Berta and I said at the same time "their gone?" "Where did they go?" I thought maybe they had gone to a motel or something. They said they had left and gone back to Texas. I thought, "Well, that figures" Here we are trying to get there, and Nancy was driving up from Virginia, and Dad leaves. I knew better than to ask but I did anyway.

And I said, "What happened now?" The guys started talking at the same time. They said Dad and Mac had almost come to blows. Did I say how come? Long before Dot had died, she made it known to every one, there was never to be any pictures made of her in her casket. And she meant it. None!!! Well, when Dad got to Ohio, he had it all set up with Linda for her to take snapshots of Dot at the funeral home. Mac must have seen her doing it, or just sensed it and asked for the film. Linda lied and said there wasn't any pictures. Mac said there was and Dad got into it, and one thing led to another until Dad threatened to hit Mac with his cane. Mac told them to get out of his house, that Dot was his wife and he would see that her wishes were carried out.

Of course, Mac was upset with Dot's dying and he told Dad if he hit him with that damn cane, he would have to hit him back. Even in death, Poor Dot didn't have peace. She couldn't have a quiet funeral. After the blow up, Dad and Linda left. They didn't even have the decency to wait for me or Nancy. They could have gone to a motel. But that would be the right thing to do.

Since it was August, I was sitting on the porch when Nancy and Wayne drove in. It was hot and muggy, which it always is in Ohio that time of year. I hadn't seen Nancy since 1970. This was 1993.

We hugged each other for a long time and just sat talking about ourselves and Dot. Then, because the funeral had already been held, we asked if they would take us to the cemetery. It was at her grave that it really hit me. I hadn't been able to say goodbye. I was never told why the funeral had been rushed so, knowing Nancy and I were trying to get there. Every one was so upset. I remembered one of the last calls I had with Dot. She said she was so tired of being sick and her mind was willing but her body was giving up. She had a lot wrong with her for only being 58 years old. I try to tell myself she isn't suffering anymore but I am because I miss her so.

Over the next few months, I would catch myself going to the phone to call her. Instead, I would call Mac. We were trying to get him talked into coming to Nevada and thought we had him talked into it. Then 11 months after Dot died, Mac killed himself. They were married 38 years. It's ironic, poor Dot had been so sick so long and wanted to live, but couldn't. And Mac could have lived but didn't.

We were going to Dayton for Mom when Holly called to tell us what happened. I told her we would be there as soon as we could. The poor girl had all that dumped her. She got it under control and got everything done. There wasn't anything I could do from out here, except give her advice. I wasn't very good at doing that stuff myself. But I was about to learn.

When we got to Dayton, I couldn't believe what I saw. Mom finally answered the door wearing 3 layers of sweat suits. I was dying of the heat, it was July. She acted like she didn't know us. When we walked into the kitchen, it was not the room she always kept. Her table was piled high with un-paid bills and there wasn't any food to speak of. She said she ate peanut butter for her breakfast. I guess that's all she could remember to eat. The thing confusing us was, she had some of her late husband's relatives living with her. They must have known she wasn't acting normal. I started right away, trying to get her bills straightened out. I couldn't believe the mess. She had been a telemarketers dream. Her house was filled with panty hose and lifetime light bulbs etc. A whole gob of useless things the marketers kept calling her about and she wouldn't or couldn't say no to. The people on the phone had her number as a mark and they talked so fast she couldn't keep up with them. So she always said yes to buying. Her phone rang constantly while we were there.

I would answer and tell them to take her name and number off the list. I can't begin to tell you all the different companies that called. I explained to them she was sick but they were heartless. They wanted their money. I told them she didn't have any. They would get nasty and threaten to sue me. I just said, "Go ahead and when it's all over I will sue you and win. I'm not your customer here." I tried to be fair with them and send a small part but they weren't satisfied with that. I told them if we went to court, I'm sure they would lose. They were scamming an old lady and one with Alzheimer's besides. I'm sure the court would start an investigation. Federal Trade Commission etc. Once we got her settled in a nursing home, I put all her bills in a box along with other papers, and put them in our truck and got ready to head to Nevada. It took me a long time to get them in any kind of order to work with them.

The so-called relatives had a lot of things at the house. They called and asked what we were doing? I told them getting ready to lock up the house, because we had turned it over to Century 21 to sell. They said, "You can't do that". I said, "Don't tell me what I can do". "If there is anything in this house you want, we will be locking the door in a week. If you want it, come and get it before that" Oh they had all kinds of excuses why they couldn't. Bad back, no truck, on and on. I said well, that's the plans. Even if you have to leave it in the yard until you get a truck, so be it. The few bills I had already looked at, I couldn't believe the credit cards hadn't been stopped and were allowed to continue without any payments. The poor thing hadn't been told she didn't have to keep paying for these leeches that were living off her rent free and were abusing her hospitality. I found hundreds of canceled checks made out to "cash" for varying amounts from $100.00 to as much as $500.00. They never bought any food from the looks of the cabinets.

Not one penny for her at least. No cleaning of her house. They were using her upstairs attic that had been built into bedrooms and storing their things in the basement. While I was trying to get a hand on her affairs, they had the nerve to tell me I couldn't do it. I told them "you just watch me. You have exactly 10 days to get your stuff out of this house. Because at that time it gets padlocked . If you have anything left inside, oh well. It will be sold when the house gets sold."

They tried several tricks on our realtor but he represented us well. The fun was about to begin. It lasted from 1994 until 2002.

The first two years were by long distance. Her in the nursing home in Ohio and after the two years we brought her out to Nevada with us, with Holly as her companion on the plane. I remember all the good times we had over the years and how her husband, Charles, at the time, always made sure there was applesauce in the house for Berta .Once Mom forgot to get applesauce for Berta. Don't know who was more upset, Charles or Berta. Then Charles died. After some time passed, Mom remarried, Cleo. From the beginning, he told Dave to stay away. He would take care of her from that time on. So for 20 years, we did as we were asked.

He made sure he isolated her from us, but he did make sure he used her as a free nurse for himself and his daughter, Shirley, who has M.S. I do not resent her helping Shirley at all, what I do resent is the fact that he and his family used her abilities and wouldn't let her visit with us.. He was a very arrogate and self-serving man. He made her drop all of us. I realize she was an adult and could have refused, but I always had a feeling she was afraid of him. Once Cleo died, she changed back to her old self. He died in 1991.

Mom wanted to take care of the girls while we went to Colorado for a deer-hunting trip one year. And in her trying to have fun with them, she literally ran herself into the ground. She had never learned to ride a bike but tried. Fell right off!!! They went for a hike. Fell in the creek!!! She pretty much banged herself black and blue. She was such a good sport. The girls loved being with her. And all of a sudden, she wasn't there after she married Cleo. He was so controlling he even talked her into eloping, like a couple of teenagers. The girls were so disappointed. They wanted to be in her wedding.

We tried to see her as much as we could but whenever we went to Dayton, he made us feel so uncomfortable, it really wasn't fun. So our time together got shorter and shorter. They came to Nevada once in 20 years. They were to stay 2 weeks but after just three days, Cleo started talking about going to California to visit with his brother. He had Mom in tears. Broke my heart when he demanded to leave early. I asked Mom why she let him treat her that way? She said it was easier and it kept the peace. I never talked to him again. Not long after they got back to Dayton, the old coot suffered a stroke. I still sent gifts to him and cards but felt nothing for him. It was for Mom's sake. After he died, we went back to Ohio and brought Mom out here with us to help her get over it. It was then that I noticed she was acting strange .by repeating a lot. But I didn't put it together. I knew nothing about Alzheimer's. If I had even suspected, we would never have put this woman on a plane by herself. We did ask for a wheelchair to be waiting for her at all landings. Thank God, she got home all right. She could have ended up in Cuba.

When the girls were growing up, we usually did things together - camping, rock hunting, deer hunting - most everything. That is why as they were growing up, they were growing away from us as well. I hated that. I guess I didn't want to let go. Berta was getting old enough for boys. Lord have mercy! Then she met Lucky. And they decided to get married. It was 3 years later that she had our one and only granddaughter, Amanda. Oh joy, I had such fun buying her pretty little girls dresses and all kinds of toys. She was the light of our lives. It was fun watching her grow. She was around adults all the time so she learned fast. Walking, talking and potty training. When she would go to the potty and finished, she would shout, "wipe me butt", no matter where she was or who was there. I thought our life was a bed of roses. Then there was a phone call from Berta asking us to come to Tennessee. She was leaving Lucky. So off we went from Arkansas to help out. By the time we got there, things had changed again. Berta had decided to stay with Lucky. So we went back home. After some time had passed, Berta did move over to Arkansas in her monster Ford LTD and little Amanda in tow. She got a job right away at the Holiday Inn. Peggy was living in Ohio with Dot and her family. I took care of Amanda. She was a hand full for sure. But I loved her to pieces. Dave was building onto our house at this time. And while he was up on the roof, he hears this little voice say, "I helped you Pappaw". And boy had she. She had mixed all sized nails together as one size. She was so proud. It took Dave hours to sort them. She would play in our yard with our dog Bouncer. That was a sight. A little 2-year-old girl and a 135 pound Doberman Pincher. She could have put a saddle on him and rode him as a pony. A very different picture from when they first met each other. She screamed and he barked. Berta said all she saw was teeth and tongue from Bouncer. The screaming and the barking went on for 3 days.

On the 4th night, Dave made everyone popcorn. Amanda got a bowl all her very own. And she began to feed it, piece by piece, to Bouncer. She didn't eat one piece herself. She kept it up until she had fed it all to the dog. From that point on, they were best friends. He was her guardian. She never tried to hurt him either. We had such fun together. Then Berta decided to put her in Day care. To help socialize her. To give her time with little kids her size. We took her the first day and Amanda cried so hard I thought she was going to shatter glass. That set the pattern for every day .It wasn't long after that, that Lucky came to Arkansas and they got back together. And every one tried to get back to normal living. Arkansas was all right but the wages were so low, we all nearly starved to death after paying our ordinary bills.

Before Lucky came to Arkansas to be with Berta and Amanda, I got a phone call from Tennessee telling about their new house burning. No body knew where Lucky was. And there was talk of bones being found in the basement in the rubble of the house. It so un-nerved me, thinking I or Dave was going to have to tell her Lucky might be dead. After an investigation, it was determined to have been started by lightening and the bones were animal. Lucky had been with his family at the time. We were so relived. A few weeks later, he came over to get back together with them.

Peggy called sometime later to say she was coming home. It seemed her and Dot weren't getting along and Berta and her were planning a surprise 25th anniversary party for Dave and I. And this was as good a time as any to come home. So we said come on but she had to get a job and pay room and board. She agreed to this. I tried to tell both the girls' life wasn't free. And their Dad was working terribly hard just to support us. You have to earn all you get.

Even though we did without as they were growing up so they could have all they wanted, it changes as you become adult. We must have made an impression, because they both work hard in their adult years. Sometimes I do think they don't listen but then I look at them and can see them using what we tried to teach them.

While we were still in Royal, Berta and I went into Hot Springs to get Amanda from Day care. We were driving down the street and Amanda was acting up pretty bad. Berta told her if she didn't straighten up, she was going to stop the car and put Amanda out. Well, little Amanda put her hand on her hip and asked very seriously, "what the hell you trying to do? Get me killed?" She was all of 2yrs. I was laughing so hard, the tears were running down my cheeks. Berta looked at me and said "Mom, stop that". That made it worse. I could just picture this little fuss budget standing on the curb. And I laughed harder.

All this time Peggy is growing and straightening up as an adult. She always held a job, even if it wasn't a big payer. Then she wanted a car. We all went into Hot Springs and went car shopping. She decided on a little yellow Volkswagen. It was a cute little thing. She drove it everywhere. One time, she and I went to Tennessee to visit Berta for a few days. The day before we left Smithville to head home, I spotted a place at the side of the road that sold yard furniture and yard figurines. I walked around for a while until I saw what I wanted. It was a cement, 2 piece, birdbath for Dave. It took us awhile but we managed to get it wiggled around until we got it into the back seat of the car. It was so heavy the nose of the car was in the air. It really hard power steering that it didn't know it had. Dave said we had put more weight into that car than we should have. But we got it home to Royal and in time for Father's Day. Of course, Bouncer thought it was his very own personal water dish. Just high enough for him to drink out of it. So we had to put it on blocks so he couldn't reach it. The bird water mad him sick.

We stayed in Royal about 3 years and we all were getting tired of not having any money to do anything. We all started talking about how good it was living out west and the difference in wages and the health benefits. After a few of these conversations, we decided to sell our place and head west again. We had our own caravan. We settled once again at Lage's Stage Stop. Chuck and Bessie welcomed us all back. We rented one of their cabins for a while. Dave and Lucky went to work for Day mines, Victoria mine, originally owned by Anaconda. The two of them rotated driving and Peggy went to work at the Stateline in Wendover. After Amanda got started in school, Berta went to work at the Goldrush, later to be bought out by the Peppermill in Wendover. She drove back and forth to Wendover everyday, rain or shine, or blizzard... She is so much like her Dad, she would be there no matter what. She and Lucky lived in a mobile home right behind us. I would take care of little miss pooh when she got home from school. The drive would kill a mule. Peggy had an apartment in Wendover. About this time, the mine choose to have a lay off. The price of copper hit rock bottom. And since Dave and Lucky were the last hired, they were the first to go. Dave's reputation as a mechanic was so well known in this area, he didn't have any trouble getting on at another mine. It was called Amselco, Broken Hills property. Everyone around this area called it Alligator Ridge because the hill looked like an alligator from a distance. He was employed at this mine and Placer Dome, which is in the same area, 20 years. He never missed a day of work.

It was eventually bought by Kennecott Copper and the final owner while Dave worked there, was Placer Dome U.S. inc. Bald Mountain mine. I think Dave started working for them in 1980. He retired February 2002. He was 71 years old. But all those years were good paying years. They were hard because being a mechanic, he worked in all kinds of weather, hot, cold, wet, dry and snowy .While he drove those un-Godly miles to go to and get home from work, we decided to find a house closer to the bus that drove all the people to the mine. It was a great big bus, like a Grey Hound. So we moved to McGill. The street right above the school and I could keep an eye on Amanda while she was waiting for her bus. I always felt better when she was on the bus headed for Lage's.

One day while we were out at Lage's , Berta told us Lucky had left her and Amanda. We asked her when this had happened? She said about 3 months ago. We were shocked. She had been out there all by herself and didn't say anything. I asked her what she planned to do? She said, "Get a divorce as soon as I have enough money." I told her I would loan her the money if she wanted. She said, "Let's go see a lawyer". And we did and she got her divorce

Peggy in the meantime was doing well in Wendover. She worked real hard and before she knew it, she was promoted to head waitress. She was living in a tiny apartment and when we decided to move to McGill, we offered her our mobile home. All she had to do was take over the payments. We couldn't afford to just give it to her. We still owed on it. She took it with the understanding she was to pay the payments to us and I would send them in. She did for a long time. She had real nice girl friends and everything was going well... We thought... Being 125 miles from us, she was basically living her own life.

She started mixing with people we didn't know. She stopped paying us what she owed on the mobile home. It was like the difference of night and day. She avoided us whenever we went to

Wendover. She finally told us she was moving to Reno. And off she went. We would go to Reno to do shopping and always made a point of leaving time to visit with her. I noticed she was changing from her old self. But nobody else said anything. Her mannerisms were so different. She had new friends. At this time, she was working for "Martha's Children" as a wardrobe mistress. They were a wonderful singing group of brothers and sisters. But it was outside influences affecting Peggy. I had always thought of Peggy being a follower. Easily led. She lived in Reno for several years and decided to move again. Hawaii this time. I can't fault her for moving so often because of our history of doing the same thing. But Hawaii??? At the same time, I told her she would have to do the visiting because she knew I wouldn't fly. I felt something was wrong. For several years, through phone calls, I was bothered by what I wasn't hearing. Dave, Berta, Fritz and I were in Elko doing shopping and having lunch together. I just came out and said, "I think Peggy is gay" You could have heard a pin drop. Then all three said at the same time, "no she's not". I said again, "I think she is" They asked me how I was going to find out. I said I hadn't figured that out yet. But everything was pointing in that direction. The strange thing is I had never been around anyone who was gay, except my stepbrother, Don. I always knew he was different. Only I never said anything to his mother, Myrtle. He died of AIDS. He lived an isolated life style too.

I finally got my nerve up while talking to Peggy on the phone one day. After she quit telling me about what was going on in her life, I just said, "Peggy, I have something I want to ask you." She said "What?" I said, "Are you gay?" And she started crying. I told her to stop crying and answer the question. She said yes, she was. She wanted to know who told me. I told her nobody had told me anything. I just knew. Wasn't sure, that's why I was asking her. I told her this was still her home and we would always love her, and she was always welcome in our home, but give us time to get used to it. That doesn't make me a good person. We, her Dad and I, have our ways of believing and living and most of all, our old-fashioned morals. It made me feel like a failure as a parent in that department. After many years, I have tried to understand, but can't approve. I have tried not to interfere in her life. I have just tried to be here for her and Berta. Peggy has had some bad accidents and had to do some struggling while she has been living in the land of Paradise. But she has always pulled herself up and gone on.

While in Texas, I always explored. I would wonder up to the army basic training area for Fort Bliss. Me and other kids would go on to the obstacle course. We did the whole thing. Barb wire, culvert pipes, swinging ropes and last but not least, the rope thing that hung over the sides of ships for men to climb down to get on landing crafts. Oh!!! That was fun!!!. I climbed and climbed and climbed some more. I was doing fine until I looked down. Oh boy, I couldn't move. I literally froze, hanging on for dear life. I don't know how long I was hanging on up there, on those ropes but after some time, a bunch of soldiers came and tried to get me to come down. I had a death's grip on those ropes. I had managed to get up about 2 ½ stories if it had been a building. It did take several soldiers, working at different levels around me to get me down. I have always had a morbid fear of heights, so I can't tell you what made me climb up there. After they got me down, they comforted me and said I'd better leave the area. After all, it was a military base.

I would do things the other two wouldn't I would go out in the desert that surrounded our neighborhood. I came home with horned toads and what we called June bugs. Big shiny iridescent green beetles. As big as a quarter. We would catch them and tie a long piece of thread on one of their back legs. We would hold the thread and let the beetles fly up over our heads. We would play with them all day. Towards nighttime, we always let them go. The next day we were out looking for new ones. We never killed them because we felt that wouldn't be right. These beetles were as big as Egyptian Scarab beetles. When we were ready to release these gentle bugs, they would fly off with the threads trailing behind them.

Or we would play out in the yard at night and catch fire flies in a jar and set them in the bedroom and watch them turn off and on. We didn't know only females, I think, glow. They were fun to watch with the lights off. And all the while, we had our dogs. In the summer, I would try to put on plays. The dogs usually had a part in them. I put a blanket across the yard and set up chairs for the audience. Then came the one-man show. Me. I was the little teapot short and stout, and my dog was the doggie in the window, or even a grand, elaborate play actor. I really liked doing that. Everyone would come over to our house. The adults would act like I was really something. Of course, I'm sure they were only enjoying a summer's evening. This was before television.

One day, we kids from the neighborhood were out in the desert playing tag or some such game, when one of the little girls got struck by a rattlesnake. We all panicked. And started running for home. Her included. Which didn't do her any good. The poor thing died. I can't remember her name for the life of me. But I know it made me a believer in my hate of snakes. But I do respect them.

All these years going by, I always thought Dave loved me as I loved him. But I started noticing things that just didn't fit my ideas of love and being a soul mate. I t had always been me learning to do things so Dave could play or do things he wanted. First, I learned to ride on the back of a motorcycle. I learned to go hunting, hiking, rock hunting or go every single weekend to motorcycle races. Flat tracks, scramble tracks, and hill climbs. He played and I babysat our kids. I really got tired of the weekend chasing. But I figured we were supposed to do things as a family. I couldn't talk to him, he would just walk away. It was his way or no way. He believed as long as he went out the door and brought home a paycheck, his responsibility was over. That was his half. He didn't believe in helping with housework. Being wife and mother, I was supposed to do everything else. House, kids, bill, his mother. I never asked him to do anything for my family but he assumed it was my job to take care of his. We brought his mother to Nevada in 1996. We were called by her neighbor about her not paying her taxes and it had been printed in the paper. We went back to Dayton and found her in an awful state. She was suffering from the onset of Alzheimer's. That awful dementia. At this stage, she was still able to recognize us but didn't want to come out west with us. So I got on the phone and found a very nice nursing home in Kettering. That was ok for a few years but very expensive and took all her money fast. She was born and raised in and around the

Dayton area and never lived anywhere else. So I got worried about getting her in a care center here. I called her every day or so but I could tell she was not doing well back there. After we got her out here, I went about 3 times a week. I would take her puzzles and what I call trash papers, for her to read. She was always happy to see me, and never, ever forgot to thank me for coming to see her

She remembered who I was for a long time. But for the first four years in the care center, I could see her going down hill mentally. She even got so she didn't know who I was. Dave would go and I would warn him not to be hurt if she didn't know him. She would get confused and think he was her brother sometimes. Even if we told her who we were, and I did that without fail, every time we got there, she never could quite comprehend who he was after awhile. In her mind, he was gone. The girls tried to visit when they were in, but she didn't know them either. She never did know Amanda or her baby. When she came down to visit with Sebastian, Mom would say he was cute but whose is he? After 4 years in this care center, we got a call from the doctoring telling us Mom was being treated for blood clots in her leg., and they were keeping an eye on her. About an hour later, a different doctor called and said they were life flighting her to Salt Lake City. I asked "why all of a sudden?" The doctor said she had gangrene in one foot. When it was over, they had amputated her left leg up to the knee. We decided not to bring her back to Ely, so I ran around again, by way of phone, and got her into another care center in Elko. This meant a 3-hour drive one way for us, but we felt better for her there. We couldn't visit as often as we wanted but we had to do what we had to do. I always felt I failed her somehow. I know I didn't. And when she died, I know she was no longer hurting or in her foggy world. She was talking about her parents at the end like it was yesterday for her. They died many years ago and Mom was 91 when she died. She would say they just left to go back to Arcanum and she had cooked a full mean for them. With that horrible condition, she lived longer than anybody in her family. Most died in their 70's .When I realized she had Alzheimer's, I watched my family members to see if I could detect any signs. Then I relaxed and said, "What will be will be".

As everyone was growing, so was Amanda. She and her mother, Berta, were living in Montello by this time. She went to a little school in the middle of town. An old rock building that must have been the first permanent building built in town. It was what was left of an old railroad town in the middle of nowhere. The teachers were exceptional and taught the kids a lot to get them ready for the outside world. Whenever she had a program, we were there, in the audience. Even though it was 189 miles one-way to be there. Usually the program lasted about 1 hour. It took 3 hours to get there, and 3 hours to get back home. Amanda started taking piano lessons about this time. She became very hard working at this and practiced all the time. She was studying classical, and she worked exceptionally hard on the Moonlight Sonata by Beethoven. She knew that was my favorite and would call me on the phone and played it for me. She was very good at it and played every chance she got. Then she started her high school years. She had to board out in Wells and go home on the weekends. Her high school was Wells High. During her 4 years, she played the piano and was into everything in school. She carried very high grades all through school. She had several boyfriends but finally settled for one whose name was Billy Hylton. They did everything together. In her senior she signed up for the Army after graduation. She was trying to decide which college to go to. They both got to go to the College of Southern Idaho. They did very well but seemed to out grow each other. And each had different goals for life. After going together all through high school and college. They decided to go separate ways. .And then there was. Gerard. Fair skinned, and red, red hair. He was a true Irishman. Came to the U.S. from Ireland. County Kilkenny. He had a very heavy Gallic accent. I had a hard time understanding him and was always saying, "What did you say?" or "huh?" They lived in Idaho.

After about 5 years, they separated and went their own ways too. I guess their problems couldn't be worked out. From what was told to us, it had something to do with having a baby. He got the house, she got the cats. After much hemming and hawing, she got around to telling us she was pregnant with our great grand son. Baby Sebastian was born Oct 23, 2001. He was a little baby, but so cute. He was always making noises. He grew like a weed. The bad part was they live so far away and we didn't get to enjoy him as much as we would have liked. He is adorable and is all boy. Being from a family of girls, it was so different. I didn't know what to buy for him. But it's getting easier. And I love him to pieces.

Amanda lived with the baby's father and didn't marry him for a long time. This is a definite going against Dave's and my ideas but we have to stand by and not say anything. We are only grandparents. One person said to me, that I have been married to Dave so long, I'm comfortable and this is the way things are done in this day and age. My answer was, "does that make it right?" We only have a few rules to live by, what's so hard?

We love them dearly and I hope they know it. But disagreeing doesn't change that. But it does not mean we approve either. There is an old saying that the apple doesn't fall to far from the tree. But I have spent my life trying to keep my mother's shadow from casting its image on me or my loved ones. I never wanted to be compared with my mother. Nothing to be proud of when it came to my mother. But in this time and place, there doesn't seem to be shame or embarrassment.

So I just watch...

Somewhere along the line, somebody decided Dave and I aren't important. Up until they died, our parents received gifts and cards and flowers. Birthdays, fathers and mothers days, Christmas, they always got something. Sometimes it wasn't big, but they got something to let them know we were thinking of them. And every time one of them was in the hospital, they got flowers. But some time someone decided we were not entitled to those things. But at the same time, I have to listen to how many miles are traveled to see a sick friend. Or I have to listen to how hard some one works to get just the right gift for a friend. When I had cancer and had two surgeries for the removal of it, not one single get-well card did I get. It was one of the most deadly types, malignant melanoma. I sat here day in and day out, half-scared out of my mind. I didn't even get anything from my Dad. But that didn't surprise me ...But it sure did hurt.

Then I went to Salt Lake City for an angiogram. And my artery opened up in my leg so I nearly bled to death in my own leg. It was a lot and very painful. This was the week before Thanksgiving. It didn't do so well and I called the hospital. This was the day before Thanksgiving by this time. They told me to get right in and to be very careful because it could be an artery and could rupture. So we went in. It turned out to be a huge blood clot. So we came home. Dave went to work on Thanksgiving Day and I stayed in the recliner with heat on it by this time. About 5 p.m. I got in the car and hobbled into the jailhouse coffee shop and bought us two dinners to go so we would have something to eat. Not even a phone call. Everyone was spending the day in Idaho. I can't tell you how hurt we were. Dave always says "its ok we take care of our selves" But you know, after awhile that gets old.

One of the biggest hurts of my life was when Berta married Lucky. We were not invited and were actually told to stay away. What do you do? You stay away and cry for three days. I know Dave was hurt to the quick. I can't say I ever got over that. I think that's when Dave decided to move again. We headed west and took Peggy with us. Now it was her turn to kick our teeth out. If there were any left for her to kick out. I don't know if there were any left after Tennessee. One day the school calls and says Peggy hadn't been in school all day. I started looking for her. Then I called Dave to have him help. She wasn't the only one missing. I finally gave up and called the sheriff's office and asked him to help look for her. I said if they found her, to hold her. They found her and called us to the office. There she was with all the little darlings. They had been getting ready to leave town. With a preacher no less. He was yammering on about all of us being bad parents, and all the while, he was going to take them to some place like Denver and sell them into prostitution. I told him to get out of my face. This, when I think of it now, was funny. He was 6 ft. tall if he was an inch. He told me not to talk to a man of God that way. I told him "if you're a man of God, God help us." Everyone there was real quiet. About that time, Peggy decided to get real mouthy with me. Dave hauled off and knocked her back into a wooden chair. It rolled across the floor and she said to the sheriff, "are you going to let him do that to me?" The sheriff said, "He's your father. He can do anything within reason" She settled right down. And the next day the chair was out on the street for the trash truck to pick up. It was broken. It's not anything we are proud of but we couldn't let her leave town. We may not have ever seen her again.

But I think I'm getting ahead of myself here. There is still more growing up together.

As I start to write down my thoughts, my mind goes back to when we were still in high school when Nancy and Dot were graduating. Nancy and Dot both looked so pretty in their caps and gowns. Maroon and white. Caps set just right on their heads. They graduated one year apart. When Dot graduated I was on my way to becoming a mother. Dad put Dot's cap on my head and told me to put her gown on so he could take my picture. He said it would be the only one he would ever get of me in a cap and gown. He didn't want any of me in maternity clothes.

Dot was working in D.C. for extra credits. It was called diversified occupation. She went to class half a day and worked the other half. The credit went toward her graduation credits. Nancy started out at

Bladensburg but graduated from Laurel high, in Laurel, Maryland. She lived with our good friends who had lived next door to us in El. Paso. The Greys. We had grown up with their only daughter, Jackie. Her Dad had been in the army with Dad. I used to try and imagine what it must be like to be an only child, with loving parents. I have to admit she was rotten to the bone. And she bossed us around like she had sergeant's stripes, but we didn't mind. We were always together. One time, Jackie was going to pierce my ears. I was ready. I had my earlobes frozen with an ice cube. I had my nerve built up and was sitting there like one big dummy and Dad happened to walk in. He asked what we were doing. We told him. He said, "Oh no you're not". So we put everything away and went on to some other kind of business. I guess he figured I could get lockjaw or blood poisoning. Or maybe he didn't want me to do it because I wanted it. I knew there wasn't any good begging him.

Nancy lived in Laurel for a while and Dot and I stayed in Landover Hills. Dad would visit with Mrs. Grey after her husband died. Pretty regular and we would go as well. Of course, Jackie was there being herself. Once, we were getting ready to eat and I was told to sit down. I asked "where?' and Jackie said, "it doesn't matter, beggars can't be choosers". I never forgot that. Nancy was staying with Jackie and her mother, I guess, because we had been life long friends and the two of them wanted to graduate together. We all went to the Laurel high school graduation in June 1953 and the Bladensburg high graduation June 1954. I would have graduated in June 1955 if I had stayed in school. But by that time, I was very busy and living in Ohio.

All the time we were living in Ohio, we had our own houses and once the guys got jobs, doing good. The army behind us and a paycheck was coming in every two weeks. We visited back and forth all the time. Dave and Mac were like brothers. Having fun together and getting in trouble together too. All of Mac's family lived in Kentucky, so he didn't have anyone, family wise, close by. The two men worked at the same place sometimes. Mac really wanted to be a farmer. He always enjoyed working in the dirt. Dot stayed at home. I don't think she wanted to work outside the home. She and I were always on the phone with each other. Then Nancy had her fill of Myrtle and came to Ohio to live with us. The three Musketeers back together again. She went right to out and got a job. She didn't have a car but paid one of the women who worked there, weekly for a ride. We were lucky to have a car for the guys to go to work in. Both were mechanics so they would glue and wire them together so they work for a while. Back then, we didn't worry about tomorrow. Day by day. As long as we had food for the baby. Young and dumb, that was us.

I remember, once in Maryland, my grandpa Lovell came to visit us. The one and only time he ever came. We all went to the Chesapeake Bay. We were making a day of it, with a picnic and lots of time in the water. I was having a really great time just staying in the water.... I was wearing shorts and a tee shirt. All at once Dad said "Gladys, get out of the water". Being trained to obey without question as I was, I didn't ask why, I just did it. Dad was standing there with a towel and he draped it over my shoulders and around me. I didn't know it then but I was the very first winner of a wet tee shirt contest. I was just starting to develop into a young lady and it showed through the wet shirt. Dad made me sit at the picnic table until I was dry. No more going into the water for me that day. That was the only clothes I had with me.

While we still lived in El Paso, my grandpa did come there once but he didn't stay long. We did go to the Carlsbad Caverns in New Mexico. I remember the trip well. I had a good time. After my grandpa went back home to Virginia, I went to a summer church camp to Fort Stockton. The only memory I seem to have about it is that I was stolen blind. I don't remember doing crafts, or swimming, which I can't do anyway, or hiking, or even Bible study. Only that I got home with very little of what I went with. Where did the commandment "Thou Shalt Not Steal" come in?

It seems like nobody wants to read my book. It's almost like I'm invisible. I ask Dave and he doesn't seem interested. He has helped me a lot with my book, trying to get it in order. I asked Berta, and she is always to busy. And Peggy is just too far away. So it seems I have blocked out any more memories. I just can't remember anything about my life this whole past year. Maybe too many serious crisis. What with my breast cancer, shingles, and nobody wanting to read it to let me know it was worth going on. It's like I'm spending an awful lot of energy doing this for nothing.

The breast cancer was such a shock. And the surgeries and the radiation treatments has made me take stock in myself. Maybe thinking nobody was interested was the wrong way to think. I went from 69 years old with nothing in between. I was the bystander. If family doesn't want to read it, how can I expect others to want to? It will be their loss.

One thing I had shoved to the back of my brain was the four years my mother had been left alone with us all alone during the Second World War. As school kids, we bought Liberty war stamps. One stamp for every ten cents. We faithfully licked and pasted the stamps into the stamp books. When the books were filled, we exchanged them for Liberty bonds. One book of stamps, one Liberty bond. For four years, we got one bond every month. We truly believed we were helping the war effort. That's a total of 144 for the three of us. If they had been allowed to mature, they would have given us a nice little nest egg when we grew up. But our mother made sure we didn't have that. She took it all. She took everything. Bonds, Dad's savings account, even our little piggy banks. She left us nothing. An adulteress plus a thief. She did leave me one thing. A memory of her that told me nobody would ever compare me to her. Lesson well learned.

In June of 2002, I had my usual mammogram. The results came back normal so I put it out of my mind. In November, I stepped into the shower and when the water hit my chest, I jumped back thinking the water was to hot, and went on with my shower. The next shower felt the same way, so I took time to think about it. The water wasn't to hot. So I did a self-exam and the fear of every woman hit me right between the eyes. I had a lump in my lump breast. I just stood there trying to calm myself and not let the fear take over. I finished my shower and went to tell Dave. I knew I had a doctor's appointment for my yearly checkup on Dec. 28th. But I moved it up to Dec.

20th. My doctor said we were going to treat it as a cyst first, and he prescribed an antibiotic, which was very expensive. Seven little pills for $150.00. I took the little jewels faithfully and refilled it once and repeated the process. It didn't seem to disappear or feel smaller. I went back to the doctor in January and told him it hadn't gone away. I said, "Is there something different we can try?" He said we can try a different pill. I took it as prescribed. Nothing. The next trip to his office, he said we were going to try an Ultra sound. I looked at him and said, "I'm not pregnant". He laughed and said the ultra sound is used for more than pregnancies. So he set up an appointment at the hospital. And off I went. The technologist doing the test, said with a certain amount of certainty, it was a cyst. In about a week I got a call from the doctor's nurse telling me the doctor thought it was a cyst but couldn't be sure. I started telling the nurse that wasn't good enough. The nurse stopped me by saying the doctor was right there and for me to talk to him personally. When he got on the phone, he went into detail of why he wasn't sure. I jumped on his case and said I wanted him to "fix" me. He said, "Gladys I am trying to fix you". And he set up another appointment.

I was pretty upset by this time. Everything we hear about the possibility of having cancer is time related. And a friend of mine wasn't doing well after being diagnosed with breast cancer. She was having a hard time with it and going down hill fast it seemed.

Everywhere I looked, I seemed to be seeing women with breast cancer. I had no one to talk to. I had to keep my panic inside and not show how scared I really was. Berta was busy with her dog shows and being Justice of the Peace. And Peggy was Peggy...Three thousand miles away…telling me all the problems her friends have and talking so fast, I couldn't get a word in edgewise.

When my next appointment came around, I asked the doctor if he would be offended if I asked for another doctor's opinion? He said "No I certainly would not be offended" and he got up and left the room. When he came back in, he had set me up with an appointment with another doctor the next day. The first thing that doctor did was order a new ultra sound with a needle aspiration. This was no fun. He said, "I know this is painful, but I have to do it one more time". I said, "Go ahead. What's a little pain among friends?" I went home.

In about three days, the phone rang. It was the new doctor. He said the results were negative. I said great, wonderful. He said he wanted me in at 3:00 p.m. for pre-op. I said, "Hey, whoa, wait one cotton, pickin minute. If the reports are negative, why do I do pre-op?" He said, "That's the problem." "You can see the lump; I can see the lump, so we need to go farther." My operation, called a lumpectomy, was scheduled for 7 a.m., April 8th, 2003. The next morning I had to be showered and shampooed by 5 a.m., I didn't do much sleeping that night.

The anesthetist was doing all the questioning. Asking about previous surgeries and I kept saying none, none, none. He asked me "you have never had any surgeries?" I said "no, none". He said I was so lucky to have gone all my life un-scathed by the scalpel. Then I told him I still had everything I was born with. He laughed and said, "I bet I know something you don't have". I asked "what?" He said "your teeth." I said "nope sorry, these are mine". He said "My God woman, do you know how lucky you are? To have all your body parts at your age."

After the surgery, I woke up with Dave holding my hand. Berta came in and said; "gosh Mom, you look great except for your hair" I bounced back quick after the surgery. Just had to kill time until the results came back, which they did. Not what I was hoping for. Cancer.

After fourteen days, I went to have the stitches removed and the doctor said I was going to an Oncologist in St. George, Utah. I went to St, George on April 23rd for an evaluation and discuss my problem. I met with Drs. McCune and Richards. Dr. McCune told me I had to have a lumpectomy several times. I finally told him "wait a minute" "I already had that, didn't I?' He examined me and continued saying lumpectomy. I told him the doctor in Ely told me I had that done already. He said give him a minute; he needed time to read my records, they had just got there. So I sat there in my BOB MACKIE designer gown waiting. He came back in and said the next step was an Axillary Dissection and after that, if it didn't go well, it would mean a mastectomy. The Axillary Dissection is the taking of glands out of the armpit and having them tested. I thought I was ready for the possibility of losing one of my breasts, but every time he said the word, mastectomy, I found myself reacting. I thought I was ready, brave and strong. But I wasn't. All my life I had to be a survivor, now most of all.

So here I was, quaking in my boots over the word mastectomy. I was told to go back to Ely and set up an appointment for the second surgery. Which I did. April 30th. I went to the hospital at 5 a.m. like before and had this surgery done. Glands were removed and tested, and came back negative. Thank God, the cancer had not spread.

Now I could move on with the treatments. We had to decide whether it was going to be chemo or radiation or both. Finally, between me and the doctors, we decided I would do radiation treatments. They would last 7 weeks, a total of 33 treatments. Dr. Richards said they would start June 2nd, 2003. Plans had to be made. Where we would stay, who would take care of Jasmine, our dog? What about our bills? How would they get paid with us out of town so long? After awhile I settled down and began to think straight. And then I could start making our plans. The first thing I did was make reservations at the Virgin River in Mesquite, NV. For their RV park so we could take our little camper down to live in. Second thing was to make up our minds about Jasmine.. She would go with us. It was going to be 7 weeks. I was afraid she would feel abandoned. I had to make sure we were in order to be gone so long. I had to find out about our mail. The post office said I had to fill out a form and put our names in General Delivery in Mesquite. Then I had to tell our post office when to start sending out mail to Mesquite. I had to think about how long it would take mail to go Mesquite so it wouldn't be late. Dave started fixing up the camper and worked very hard to make it comfortable and ready. He put in an air conditioner, a small microwave oven and built a shelf for a T.V. He also added a VCR so we could watch movies. He fixed my bed at one end of the camper so I could rest after my treatments. Everything he had gotten off the internet for me to read, said I would probably sleep a lot.

The air conditioner was over my head at one end of the bed. A friend asked if we needed an air conditioner and I told her no, thank you. She said if we did, she would be glad to loan us a little one she had because she wasn't using it. We had decided to take Jasmine with us because we didn't want to leave her that long. She might feel we had abandoned her.

So we were ready. We headed off on Sun. June 1st. We noticed the closer we got to Mesquite the hotter it was getting. For the entire time we were in Mesquite, the temperature ranged between 120 and 125 degrees. The hottest it had ever been recorded. Every morning we got up and headed for St. George, which was 40 miles away. My treatments would take about 15 minutes after the first time and they got me tattooed. After that was done, all they had to do was set the machines on the marks and it was over quickly... This went on for 33 treatments, 5 days a week. The people in the Oncology dept. were wonderful they would joke and treat you like a person, not a number. They always greeted me by my first name and always encouraged me. I asked if I could take some pictures of everything and everybody, including the doctors and they said, "Yes it's yours". So I got busy everyday and took pictures of everything. After my treatment for that first day, I went back to the camper and put an X mark on the calendar. One day done. I remember when I put the first mark on the day, I said "only 32 more to go". Surprisingly enough, the time went by very fast. We broke up some of the time by coming to Ely for two weekends. One was the 4th of July. And we went to Wendover, NV, and spent the day with the kids. It was so hot we decided to take my friend up on her offer to borrow her air conditioner so we had two of them.

We had decided to wait until after dark to come home after my last treatment, when it was a little cooler. Well, by that time, we were ready to come home. So as soon as we were done in St. George, I looked at Dave and said lets go home. He said, "Let's do". We went to the camper and put everything in place. And we came home. It took some time to recover but I didn't push it. I had been told it would. Everyday I got stronger. Now I have to continue to take my cancer pills for 5 years and hope for the best.

When I first met the doctors in St. George, I told them I had all the confidence in the world in them, but I had one request to ask of them. They asked me what it was? I said I had to make it to Sept. 8th. That was our 50th anniversary. And I did plan on being there. We were going to re-new our vows. They fulfilled their promise to me.

After we finished in St. George and Mesquite and got home to Ely, I concentrated on getting my strength back so Dave and I could celebrate. My breast was healing very well and the armpit where the glands had been removed for testing was coming along as well. Still numb and tender but I was able to live with it.

In the mean time, I had a brain storm... We wanted Berta, as Justice of the Peace, to perform the ceremony for us to re-affirm our vows. When I asked her, she said yes, that she would be happy to do it, as an honor to us. I remember back when Dave and I got married in 1953, I said then that if we were alive, we would have another ceremony to re-new our vows on our 50th Anniversary. I really wanted family there but they all had plans. So it was history repeating itself. It was just Dave me Berta and Fritz plus one witness from Montello.

It was the real thing, just like before. I had gotten a license from the courthouse in Ely. Which the clerk of courts gave us as a gift along with her congratulations. Berta had picked out a very lovely vows for us. Fritz was official photographer. God bless him, he did a great job. He had 3 different cameras hanging around his neck and he was kept busy taking shots from different angles. We stood by their fishpond in their front yard. After awhile, Berta and Fritz said they were taking us into Wendover and they were buying us an anniversary dinner. We went to the Rainbow Casino and to the buffet. It was a very good dinner. We all had a good time and left full. And now we are going into our second 50 years...

I sit and start thinking about how my life has made so many twists and turns over the years. And of all the different forks in the road that have been put in front of me and how I have picked the ones I have...

As a child, I didn't know right from wrong. But without knowing, I seemed to pick the right one for me. In my teens, I found the man I was going to spend my life with. I didn't have a role model to follow with either of my parents. I struggled with my self-esteem but never once did I doubt that I couldn't take care of my babies or my husband. Oh yes, I was strict with them. In fact, I was the "meanie" in our family. I was the one would did the punishing. Dave was always the good guy. But I took my marriage vows as a sacred oath. And my job as a mother just as sacred. I always felt it was the most important contract I ever signed in my life. And, by becoming a mother, God had given me two tiny lives to maintain and keep healthy.

One ordinary day, Berta called to talk on the phone. After we had gotten all the small talk out of the way, out of the blue, she slips this little sentence in, "I'm married and I have a boyfriend" and keeps on talking hoping I hadn't heard it. I finally got her attention, by saying "stop" several times. I asked her what she had just said. She said, in a quiet way, that it was over with Fritz. Of course, I was dumb founded. I must say I was floored. I got myself together and asked why? What had happened to bring this on? She began to talk, slowly, and she said it hadn't been right between them for almost 4 years now. I told her we thought everything was great with them because they had gone on that extended dog show vacation in June, that it was o.k. with them then. When they got back, she had praised Fritz for all his help with the dog equipment. So, I must say, it was a surprise. She kept saying how great Fritz was.

But then everything shatters. I couldn't seem to grasp what she was saying. Then I started to listen... She was saying she was tired of being unhappy. She wanted a man to take care of her for a change. She was tired of living alone. That part I understood. ...I told her I knew what she was talking about because Dave had lived at the mine the last 4 years before he retired. I didn't like it myself. But over all our married life, I was the one left to pay the bills, that the girls were taken care of and all was well on the home front. You know small things like getting kids to school and dogs to the vets, etc. Just small things in general, that makes up married life. Nobody told me what it was, I just did it.

I asked her what the real reason was? Then she broke down and told me Fritz had betrayed her trust with a "friend" of hers. I told her it was hard to believe of Fritz. I wasn't doubting her at all. But it was a surprise.

My mind wandered back to those 4 years and I remember she was having trouble with their life together and staying with Fritz then. She was very upset and was going to leave him then but I told her to hang in there and try to work things out. She never told me the whole story of the problem then, so I thought it was only a bump in the road. I told her it was hard to believe that of Fritz. I wasn't saying what she was telling me was a lie. But I swear, for him to have sex with Liz, boy, now that's really desperate. I always want my girls to know I love them, and stand behind them no matter what they choose to do, within reason. But I cannot condone breaking the commandments. Not that I'm a saint myself, but can't do that and live with myself.... Needless to say, I was most distressed when I found out our Amanda had committed adultery, and now my oldest daughter is doing the same thing. With no conscience.

I know she knows her ten commandments. She went to church as a child. And number 7 is one of them... I am very upset and I try not to be. She says in a haughty manner, she will do whatever it takes. And evidently, no matter who it hurts. This is sad because I told her she has already tarnished her soul. She is 50 years old and I can't protect her soul any longer. I told her she probably won't go to Heaven... She said she doesn't believe in that. I said how convenient. I told her it was much easier to say, "I don't believe" just so you can break the rules and do whatever you want without fearing the consequences. I want her to be happy, but there is a right way and a wrong way to do it. It's called a divorce first. The man is wrong too. He knew she was married. But he coveted his neighbor's wife. I am sorry to say, I told her it probably won't last. Because of the way it's being done. She said to me I had taught her and Peggy to be independent. I said yes I did, but I didn't teach her to commit adultery. She said, "I know that".

It took me and Dave some time to come to grips with this. We discussed it over and over. He gave me his ideas and I gave him mine. The strange thing is, when all is said and done, we were saying the same things, in different ways. All my life, I have always tried to be a good person. I believe in my God. Dave has never said much about what he believes in. He has never tried to stop me from going to church, or watching religious shows on T.V. or reading the Bible. He was right there to say we were going to get married in a church in Maryland. He has said he didn't believe in the Bible because it was written by a man. I always said, "Yes it was but dictated by God". "We live 10 simple rules set down by God". He must believe even a little bit because he uses them as his guidelines too. He says that while he was growing up with his grandparents, his granny dragged him to church. It was always such an ordeal for him that he gave up the church.

But I still think he believes in his heart. He was so disappointed when he found out Peggy's different way of life. And when Berta started living in out right, bold faced, adultery, his heart was broken. He said, "I don't know what our kids want from us". "They keep saying everybody's doing it". "Well I don't believe it". It's a sin no matter how you sugar coat it. One day I saw him sitting, just staring out into space He had tears in his eyes. I asked him what was wrong, and he said, "Why don't our kids like or want to be with us?" I said "I don't know" "I guess we are too old fashioned" It is always expected that Dave and I accept it all.

Dave and I did decide to try and get along, so we made plans to meet up in Wendover for Thanksgiving. As usual, we all gathered at the Rainbow Casino. Berta had warned us that Mark, her new love, was going to ask us to his house for Christmas at the Gamble ranch. One of his daughters and her husband camp up from Las Vegas to join us for Thanksgiving. All went well. There were eight of us adults, and our 2 great grand babies. There was the first meeting un-comfortable feelings but as we spent time together and as we were eating, it faded. We did go to Montello and Mark's home for Christmas. And we did have fun. Mark was a gracious host. He turned his home over to all the insane members of our family. For dinner, we had two extra guests. Two of the ranch hands didn't have family to spend the day with. Robert and John. Everything turned out just wonderful. Including Berta's new coconut pecan cake. As always, there was too much food. While there, we drew names for the next years Christmas

The weatherman played a trick on us that year. A blizzard came in, hard and fast. The power went out so we brought out lamps and flashlights. We had our camper so we used our propane stove to cook. We pretended we were camping. The kids were having fun. Had to keep putting oxygen in the fish tanks with hand pumps. What a time.

As of June, Berta no longer lives in Nevada. She and Mark have found a place to live in Idaho. The ranch he was working for fired him and everyone who worked for them. So he is off looking for a new cowboy job. Me and Dave are the only ones left in Nevada now. We will adjust to this too. We do wish them both good luck at starting their new life together. She will be living closer to Amanda and the kids now, which is good to a point. Now that Dave is having a medical problem, I wish they were closer for support. BUT!!!

Also, while there, I told Berta I had made a decision. It was time to let go. If they fall down, they have to pick themselves up, dust themselves off and try to go on. It doesn't mean we don't love them for themselves, it just means it's time for Dave and me. My cancer had brought me face to face with my mortality. And it is definitely time for us.

My mind starts thinking about my life, all 69 years of it, and no matter what I do, it will not stop. It runs like a movie projector. Even when I think I have wrung everything out of it, like a sponge, there is always more to think about. It comes all at once and I have to stop and pull out one thought at a time to make sense of the jumble.

Today I was reading my medical records having to do with my breast cancer. It's been almost three years since my surgeries and radiation treatments. I was surprised at the old fear that washed over me. I have been diligent with doctor appointments, mammos and checkups every six months. I take my cancer pill everyday. My mentality has always stayed up because the doctors say keep happy thoughts, and stay away from stress. Boy, now that's a challenge.

In Aug., of 2004, I joined the Red Hat Society. The ladies are all a blast to visit with. All over 50 years of age. We have all been there, said that and done it. So no rules.

We have a monthly luncheon and enjoy learning about each other. As the ladies asked me about me, some of my thoughts take me back to El Paso and me trying to learn to swim at Fort Bliss swimming pool or trying to roller skate on a very short piece of sidewalk. Life seems to be a long line of chapters. Each one opening and closing. One step at a time. Left foot, right foot. And without knowing when it happened, you're into a new phase of your life. But the earlier part of my life are filed away, just waiting to pop into the front of my memories, like it happened yesterday. Some happy. Like calling my Dad "Willie" just to get him to chase me through the house. Happy times like for a little girl, my Dad wasn't going back to war. Happy times like Christmas, Easter, and birthdays.

I woke up one morning in med August feeling like a ton of bricks fell on me. Every bone and joint in my body hurt, bad. I mentioned it to Dave and said I thought I had the flu. He said he didn't think I was coming down with the flu. This was about the 18th or 19th. On Sunday morning, Aug. 21st, I was getting dressed for the day, when I looked into the mirror. My left buttock was covered with a mess of blisters and a purple rash. Huge blisters. I called Dave in to look at it. He took a long look at it and said these dreaded words. "Well, Babe, you have the Shingles". I said how did he know that this was that? By this time, I was in such terrible pain. Every nerve on my left side was telling me it was affected. The entire left buttock, all around the panty line and the whole left side of the pubic area. Sitting, standing, showering, lying in bed or sitting on a chair, was plain agony. Every time I moved, I hurt. The worse was going to the bathroom. Depression hit me very hard. I was given very strict orders by the doctor not to watch any 911 scenes on T.V. or none of the flooding in New Orleans brought on by hurricane Katrina.

There were other southern states hit hard by the storms. There wasn't any sleep at night, I couldn't eat. Twice Dave took me to the emergency room I was so bad. It was affecting my heart.

Couldn't keep any food down. All part of the agony. I would stand in the shower and cry so Dave wouldn't hear me. I went to the doctor to see how long the misery was expected to last. He said I wouldn't even begin to feel any relief until after 6 weeks had passed. I told him that's not what I wanted to hear. Every morning I got out of bed, stood there, and waited for the pain to come. Then after about 6 weeks, I could tell I was getting a little better. One smidge at a time. As I'm writing this, 6 months have gone by. I learned early, the trick was, Don't Move. Sit in a recliner, very quiet. If you move, the nerves tell the muscles what to do. And if the nerves do the telling, the hurt starts with no mercy. Dave found some homeopathic spray and oil on the internet that did some relief. They were very expensive but worth every penny in relief. I had a 6 months appointment in St. George for my cancer checkup, so we had to drive down. We took the oil and spray with us. As the pain got to bad, Dave would find a deserted side road and I would take down my slacks and panties so Dave could spray me and we could go on a little farther.

Many a time my mind wanders back to the days when I was a very small child. Different acts of cruelty or kindness, which shape your life. I may not have known it at the time, but have come to realize it now. Back in the 1930's and 40's or beyond, people, adults, never interfered with what parents did or did not do to their children. Most babies were accidents. The adults had babies and considered them just another mouth to feed. I think I have grown into a more considerate adult because of my rough childhood.

As Dave and I have gone through the years of our life together, we have gained, totally lost everything and regained to start over. My sister Dot would never let go of anything. Any possession, once she got it, was her's forever. It meant security to her. Whether it was clothes, animals, husband, house, or her children.

I hear on the news about adults abusing their children or worse, murdering them. I used to have thoughts go through my mind all the while Rose was beating us or tormenting us to our limits. "She is going to kill us". I am surprised she didn't. I never will know what stopped her.

You see, our daughters were raised in a safe family atmosphere. Never feeling un-loved. As Dave and I were. His mother had him at a time , when, if a girl got pregnant outside of wedlock, she would be disowned and usually sent to a make believe sick Aunt in a distant town for the remaining days until she delivered. Then the girl would come back home with some wild tale of how her Aunt had recovered. Not only did the family disown her but friends and church did too. So when Dave's mother went into labor with him, she was still claiming she wasn't pregnant. Her father told me this story with his own lips. She had Dave at her parents farm. After she had him, she turned him over to Granny and Dad to raise. She went back to her life as a nurse in Dayton. At that time the 30 or so miles from the farm to Dayton was a pretty good stretch People back then didn't have cars or transportation to go very far. So she figured she was safe from prying eyes. Never once while he was growing up, did he live with his mother. His parents were his grandparents. Even though she married three times, she never had him live with her and her husbands. I figured out her motto, "out of sight out of mind" She even told me once, "don't mention Dave's not having a father." Because Cleo, husband of the day, doesn't know anything about this". Like Cleo hadn't known about Dave not having a father. And after all, his name is Gartrell, same as mom's maiden name, and the same as Granny and Dad's last name. Give me a break!!!

There were time after my two daughters were born, that I thought my heart would explode with the love I feel for them. If anybody and I mean anybody, had tried to hurt them or take them away from me, I might have done almost anything to keep them from harm. I grew up with them and am guilty of keeping them to close to my breast. But I wanted to take all their pain and hurts away if I could. As they grew, I came to the decision we can't wrap them in cotton batting and not let them see the ways of the world. Sometimes it's a horrible place but most times, it's a good place if you want to see it.

Gladys Lovell Gartrell, author of *Three Little Girls Lost*

www.ingramcontent.com/pod-product-compliance
Lightning Source LLC
Chambersburg PA
CBHW061258280526
45784CB00002B/812